HENRY'S CHRISTMAS

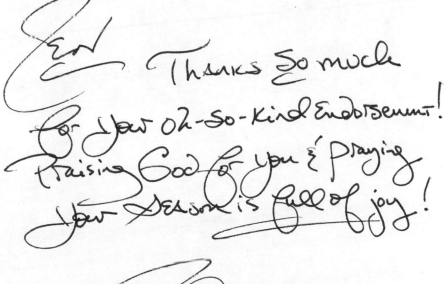

Thanks so much for your oh-so-kind Endorsement! Praising God for you & praying your season is full of joy!

HENRY'S CHRISTMAS

A Story for Discovering God's
Joyous Work at Advent

JOHN ELTON PLETCHER

CROSSLINK
PUBLISHING

Henry's Christmas: A Story for Discovering God's Joyous Work at Advent

CrossLink Publishing
www.crosslinkpublishing.com

ISBN 978-1-63357-082-5

Library of Congress Control Number: 2016947217

EARLY REFLECTIONS

"As an architect feeling the same kind of pressures, market cycles with uncertainties, and similar relational challenges, I was drawn into reconsideration about being more intentional in this coming Advent season. This story relates a realistic journey of the work-a-day life. When challenging people break into our story, especially in a season calling us to charity and grace, one can encounter the need for Advent in a fresh way. In the midst of this busy season, *Henry's Christmas* unlocks new perspectives and possibilities, providing mystery, intrigue, and new considerations for mission. And most of all, Christ is in the middle of it all!

Inspirationally written, this engaging story urges personal assessment of one's own faith-in-the-marketplace opportunities and a challenge to reach beyond. And in the end, it will leave you wanting for more!"

—Dale R. Yoder
AIA, President, Cornerstone Design Architects

"Henry's back, and this time he takes us on a Christmas road trip that shows just how human the characters in the Christmas story really were—and how much we resemble them. *Henry's Christmas* will help you and your family explore the Christmas joy that grows from embracing the wonders of God's work in the lives of real people who were open to receiving and serving him."

—Dr. James R. Lytle
President, Clarks Summit University

"*Henry's Christmas* tells of a remarkable truck—er, *trek*—using 'story' to move us from pre-grumpy Christmas blues to a place where faith and Christmas feel innocent, fresh, and exciting again. Weaving delightfully realistic 21st century characters into an intimate exploration of the delightfully realistic 1st century people involved in Jesus' birth, the author creates a tapestry that not only entertains us but also models creative ways to carry Jesus from past to present until He is once again a visible part of *our* everyday journeys."

—Randy Kilgore
Writer for *Our Daily Bread* and author of *Made to Matter: Devotions for Working Christians*

"*Henry's Christmas* captures all the favorite sights and sounds of the Christmas season while encouraging deeper exploration of courage, kingdom anticipation, joy, and generosity. John Pletcher writes in a very simple story format that is layered with complex concepts, motivating toward meaningful action. This book will challenge you to evaluate your own response to the Advent season and will inspire you to utilize your God-given gifts for kingdom impact in the local community and around the world."

—**Jen Beachy**
Program Manager, Joni and Friends Eastern PA

"The bookcases of most leaders are full of books on faith, work, and charity. But few of these books are as fun to read as *Henry's Christmas*. In this festive tale, John Pletcher explores life's most important questions—and our deepest longings— through the lens of a story. This spirited book is a fresh and engaging guide to the Advent season."

—**Chris Horst**
Vice President of Development, HOPE International, author of *Mission Drift*, and founder of dadcraft

DEDICATION

Dedicated with deepest honor and fondest memories to my grandparents, Janet and Everett Hall. At a very early age, I learned that Christmastime could be full of wonder, anticipation, and all-out joy. As I was growing up, my grandparents indulged our family in delightful décor, scrumptious baking, and oh-so-generous, often surprising, gifts. Though many other family members and friends have contributed to my love for Christmas, Grandma and Grandpa Hall indelibly etched a passion for the season on my soul. I am confident that they would enjoy this story and these stirrings toward greater joy!

CONTENTS

INTRODUCTION

The Work of Christmas

Humongous humbug or jubilant joy? Which one most readily describes how Christmas commonly feels for you, your coworkers, clients, family, and friends? The story in your hands was written as a hopeful antidote to the all-too-typical stress, the mad dash, and messy malaise that normally characterize our workplaces, homes, and neighborhoods during the holiday season.

Enjoy this four-week journey of discovery along with Zach, Maggie, old Henry, and a colorful collection of other characters. Get ready to personally discover how faith-filled courage, kingdom anticipation, jubilant joy, and gracious generosity transformed the ancient cast of original Christmas characters over two thousand years ago—and how these same discoveries can transform your own Christmas season this year.

The twenty-five chapter story was designed for personal inspiration, daily reading with family, or discussion along with friends in your small group or class. Stretching across this marvelous time of Advent, each week contains a cluster of story chapters followed by various questions, Scriptures for further research, and suggested exercises to enrich your soul.

A word of explanation might prove insightful—and hopefully empowering. *Henry's Christmas* is an anticipated sequel to *Henry's Glory*. Typical of most tales, I concluded the first story with two simple words: THE END. However, very quickly after its publication, excited readers began emphatically saying to me, "What happened next? That can't *truly* be the end." Hence, you are holding the next key movements of discovery for our small band of adventurers. Rest assured if you did not yet read the first one, you can still trek along quite confidently and enjoyably on the journey. (No previous reading is required, and you can always backtrack later to read the first one.)

In the wondrous spirit of this blessed Advent season, you are warmly invited to enter this story. Dare to discover how courage, anticipation, joy, and generosity can work God's wonders for your own Christmas and beyond. Turn the page and embark on the adventure!

John Elton Pletcher
Lancaster, Pennsylvania
Summer 2016

ADVENT WEEK 1: DISCOVERING FAITH-FILLED COURAGE

CHAPTER 1

Glory Days

Glowing green, brilliant red, and golden yellow danced in the windy, flurry-filled air along Main Street. Classic traffic lights dangled mid-road, accenting similar bright colors that were festively adorning the lamp poles. From a newcomer's view, the tiny Ohio town might seem frozen in time. Frosty windowpanes displayed toy trains, elves, and vintage lanterns. Zach, however, was no stranger to this strip of road, having driven it during numerous journeys to his grandma's house. Several quaint shop windows framed shimmering, winged angels that were flying from invisible wires.

On this particular drive, the blustery air carried a unique vibe. For the thick-haired twenty-something, there was a blend of heaviness, fear, and anticipation. Thanksgiving eve, almost ten o'clock, and he was still an hour from arriving at

Gram's. Zach was driving solo in his 1977 Ford F-100. Exiting from the interstate, he was using more caution. Flurries proved to be thicker now as he drove through the little towns along Route 13. As he rolled into Bellville, the snow was noticeably heavier, blanketing the two-lane road, potentially creating more treacherous conditions.

The previous summer, Zach had inherited this old, rattily pickup from his grandfather just a few days before his death. Though the truck was fraught with mechanical issues, Gram's folksy, grease monkey neighbor, Marshall, had generously performed the necessary restoration projects. Thankfully, the old fella had proven roadworthy enough to venture back to Zach's residence in Valley Forge, Pennsylvania.

Zach's very special friend, Maggie Brinkley, had affectionately dubbed the old Ford truck "Henry." Together, Zach, Mags, and Henry had gone on summertime adventures of deeper personal discovery. In subsequent weeks of grieving Grandpa's death, Zach and Mags asked soul-searching questions about the significance of their own daily work. They discovered how God's mission for redeeming people could integrate with their everyday work and motivate them to lovingly serve others. Thick conversations were laced with even thicker flirtation. Family and friends could readily surmise something was moving them past the friend zone. There was an undeniable growing endearment for one another.

But that was last summer back in Ohio, during those quintessential glory days involving Grandma's house, close family, and new friendships. They had indulged in coffee and robust theological talks with Grandpa's old, wise friend, Doc Ben. A handful of leaders at Gram's church had urged Zach to consider getting involved in Haiti. After the horrific earthquake, people in Haiti needed help to rebuild their homes, families, and whole communities. Teams had been working to restore lives, cultivate work skills, and develop a stronger cultural framework. Leaders from that team challenged Zach: "Join us on one of our trips! Come work to build new businesses and expand Christ's kingdom in Haiti."

Both Doc Ben and Gram's wrench-turning neighbor, Marshall, had wonderfully encouraged Mags and Zach. "Gain God's perspective for your work endeavors and more gracious love for others. You can bring Christ's greater glory in all you do and say each day!"

Resuming the daily grind in Valley Forge, Zach and Mags were eager to implement such new views, to genuinely love clients and coworkers, and glorify God in their workplace tasks. But now, back to their full-time labors—Zach as an architect, Mags as owner of a veterinary clinic—they quickly found their best intentions were fraught with rascally risks and bigger setbacks than they had anticipated.

During the early weeks of fall, they had continued to enjoy each other's close company, going out together more often on the weekends. Romantic sparks had continued to fly. Since Zach was employed by Brinkley Design-Build—yes, Maggie's father, Larry, owned and led the firm—the young love birds found plenty of excuses to hang out together after work and on the weekends. Mags' dad was personally intrigued that something romantic was kindling between his daughter and one of his young, star architects.

With thick-falling snow, Zach tested his truck brakes on Bellville's slick, snow-covered roads. Henry's brakes were functioning famously, with only a slight indication of potential for fishtailing. Zach was thick in thought, pondering the tangled mess of previous days. *Why did Mags have to act that way last Friday?* Zach wondered. *I sincerely thought this was blooming into a sweet and beautiful relationship.* Something had suddenly turned chilly between them. Just ten days ago, he had been seriously contemplating how she might indeed be *the one* for him. He had begun thinking about the potential of popping the question, including what, when, where—all those marvelous details that so readily triggered in his details-oriented, architectural brain.

But that was before last Friday. The previous week had proven to be ridiculously stressful at the architectural firm. Time-sensitive deadlines for pushy clients had the whole team frazzled way beyond the normal levels of chaos in the office. The holiday season's extra-full schedules and Zach's own financial demands only accentuated the stress and pressure.

Money was tight, and he couldn't help but worry. Would he have enough to buy presents and truly make this Christmas a merry one?

As a result, personal fuses were short, and Zach was struggling to remain calm, cool, and collected. Terse conversations abounded, especially with Alex, one of Brinkley Design-Build's newest employees. He was a year younger than Zach, not even close to as gifted in architectural design. And he was overwhelmingly cocky. Alex's very presence was annoying to Zach on his best days, and utterly exasperating on too many others.

Zach had attempted to fill the eight hours of silence in Henry's cab with a mix of Christmas tunes. Seasonal jazz, a cappella Pentatonix, Michael Bublé—even some classic crooners—managed to supply intermittent respite from his jumble of financial fears and workplace worries. *It would be so nice to actually have that glowing Christmas feeling starting here at Thanksgiving and carrying right through Christmas Day and into New Year's.* He had SO hoped that this Christmas season would feel different—more joyful—an emotional lift to him and his whole family after Grandpa's passing last summer. And he certainly wished his work endeavors could take on a different tone.

As he drove, a song would grab his attention, pleasantly distracting him from his jumble of internal turmoil. Then a rogue thought would jar him back to reality. The firm's work environment felt so tense and lacking purpose once again. Throughout this fall he had come to seriously adore Mags, thanks to long walks amid colorful trees as well as long talks over coffee or tea in quaint suburban cafés. But something had suddenly changed in her vibes toward him. Even their quick call today as he got on the turnpike was awkward. *I'd feel better if she had told me she would be missing me.* His thoughts were conflicted and full of regret. *Why couldn't she have said, "I'll be thinking about you and wishing I was with you for tomorrow's Thanksgiving festivities"? Or why didn't I think to say that to her?*

Zach jolted back to his icy-road reality. He had been on autopilot and was now sitting at the final red light on the edge of Bellville. Henry was idling, eager to jump off the line. Instinctively, Zach realized that Henry's tires might spin in the thickening snow, so he knew he should go easy on the gas. He glanced in his rearview mirror. Stunningly, he saw what was headed toward him. A very large pickup truck, sporting raised tires and a big-bite front grill, was barreling toward Henry. Though the foreboding truck was careening their direction, the events in the mirror were all happening much too fast for Zach to react.

The Godzilla-like pickup was skidding, fishtailing, and certainly not successfully stopping. It seemed bound to take a bite out of Henry. Zach had just enough time to grip the wheel and dig his feet into the floorboards. He braced for impact.

CHAPTER 2

Bubba of Bellville

Godzilla truck was not stopping. In fact, the big-barrel beast gathered speed on the snow-covered road. It skidded, fishtailed more, and ferociously slammed into Henry's rear bumper. Zach felt his whole frame lunge forward. Fortunately, the long-bed old truck absorbed the worst of the blow.

Glancing to his right and seeing a small gas station parking lot, Zach immediately pulled in to assess the damage. The gigantor pickup followed suit. As Zach stepped out, he reached back to massage his neck. *'Going to be a bit sore tomorrow morning, but my head is still attached. And no blood, thank God! Now what about Henry?* Zach could not help but wonder how the old fella had held up.

Stepping to the rear, he surveyed the damage. Amazingly, there was only a slight crumple in the lower center of his tailgate, just below the white FORD lettering. And some black paint mixed with scratches on Henry's rear bumper, remnants of Godzilla's teeth. Though he had managed a bite, the damage was marvelously minimal. Zach had always taken a sense of macho pride over how solid, ruggedly formidable Henry's grey steel bumper appeared. Now there was proof that the bumper's performance matched its appearance. Zach grinned and gave Henry a pat on the tailgate.

"Watch out!" a frantic female voice shouted from across the parking lot. "Bubba will get you!" Zach turned to behold a mammoth young man tumbling toward him.

"Whatta ya think you're doing in my town, ya little twerp? How DARE you mess up my truck!" Zach suddenly realized that half a dozen additional vehicles had filled in the parking spots around Henry and Godzilla. "LOOK at this, kid, 'front grill and bumper of my Chevy are a mess." A gaggle of cackling young people piled out of the sundry cars and trucks. Obviously, Bubba and Godzilla had a posse of friends along with them.

As he stepped closer to Zach, Bubba started laughing uncontrollably and pounding his left fist into the palm of his right hand. Zach stepped back. *Oh my word, this guy towers over me.* His mind was spinning, scrambling for best options. *There's no way I can go one round with this guy. No way. And he's obviously drunk as a skunk.* Though Bubba was still several feet away, the smell of alcohol wafted through the icy air. His breath was abominable.

"Bubba, STOP it!" Zach recognized the voice, the same frantic female of just moments ago. Suddenly, she was grabbing one of Bubba's arms just as a young guy grabbed the other arm, making their best attempt to pull him back.

"Your truck hit MY truck!" Zach proclaimed with short-breath bravado. Bubba's handlers looked stunned. Zach froze and looked as shocked as anyone. *How could I be so foolish to let that fly?* Bubba snorted and pulled, attempting to free himself from their tight grip.

"Listen, I don't want to fight you," Zach announced as he took five steps back. "We can make this right if we just talk about it." Bubba roared with louder laughter, spewing an even thicker scent of beer breath into the frozen, still flurrying air around them.

Zach was suddenly cognizant of the fact that the parking lot was full of Bubba's friends. The whole gaggle had apparently been doing some early Thanksgiving partying at a local watering hole. "Listen, we're trying our best, mister," the young woman pleaded, "but you need to know you don't want to mess with Bubba, especially when he's drunk." Quickly gathering his wits, Zach side-stepped around Henry, jumped in the passenger door, slid across his bench seat, and slammed down both door locks. Cautiously, he rolled his window down by an inch and proceeded to converse.

"So, if you'll just give me your insurance information, I can be on my way." The crowd roared like wild hyenas.

"He wants insurance, folks!" Bubba shouted mockingly to his crowd of supporters. "I ain't giv'n out no insurance. It's my pap's truck. Not sure he's even got any!"

Zach pumped the gas, turned the key, and Henry rumbled to life. Putting it in DRIVE, Zach announced through the window, "Okay, okay, I'm out of here!" Bubba lunged forward—his handlers could no longer hold him back—and he began pounding his fists into Henry's hood. The posse let out an audible cheer. Zach cranked the steering wheel to his right, mashed on the gas pedal, and laid down rubber as he sped out of the parking lot.

Every nerve in his body was on high alert. Adrenaline was rushing. *Did that really just happen? As if I didn't already have enough stress and shock to my system. So much for happy holidays!* Zach pondered to himself with his typical snarky comments. He kept checking his rearview mirror. Nothing coming—*relief*—no one was following. The snow was lighter now, but he was still cautious. After about ten miles, Zach let up on the gas as he rolled around the edge of Fredericktown. His blood pressure had begun to descend and his normal senses were returning. *Unbelievable! Just my luck—the perfect way to begin the most wonderful time of the year.*

Just then, he noticed a small brick church on the left side of the road. He pulled in and reached for his phone in the glove box. *Who do you call when you've just experienced such a surreal ambush?* Zach wondered. Tapping *Favorites*, he pressed *Gram*. Two rings and she answered.

"Hello, Zachary. Everything okay? We've got flurries falling here." Grandma was forever the worrier.

"Yes, Gram, I'm all in one piece. All safe, but you'll never believe what just happened to me. Suffice it to say, I've gotten delayed, but I'm on my way. Get ready. Brew some hot tea, please. Do I have a story to tell you! I should be there within the hour."

"Fine, fine, Zachary. You drive careful now. I will start the water on the back burner." Zach knew he did not dare tell Gram anything more until he had safely arrived back in the driveway. If she heard the whole tale over the phone, she'd be calling 911 and ordering a police escort.

Snowflakes were larger and falling heavier now. As he dropped his phone on the seat bench, he noticed a peculiar light emanating from the front side of the church's red brick. Putting Henry in DRIVE, Zach headed toward the mysterious light.

Tucked amid a short alcove of pines was a weathered, dusty-white nativity scene. They were all there. Zach took careful inventory—Mary, Joseph, shepherds, a sheep, a donkey, and three wise men—each of the leading characters. Had there been no snow, they would have been more visible. Zach pulled closer and rolled down his window.

They looked so tranquil in their statuelike poses, yet oh-so-purposeful. Joseph's face was confident. Mary appeared reflective. Zach suddenly realized how uniquely curious he felt toward the holy entourage. With his architectural penchant for detail, he observed the plaster construction, or perhaps it was ceramic. He was uncertain. With the fresh-falling snow, they gave the illusion of exquisite snow sculptures. Somehow, the artist had captured very specific expressions. The shepherds had determined looks, like they might be about to embark on some new adventure of great consequence. Two small, angelic creatures graced the top of the crèche. Their faces exuded radiant joy.

Zach mused. *If anyone needs a dose of what those chubby cherubs have this season, it's certainly me.* He shook his head.

Aiming Henry's wheels back out onto Route 13, he headed for Gram's house and—in no way he could possibly foresee—a Thanksgiving weekend full of adventuresome insights and future-shaping surprises.

CHAPTER 3

A Grand Thanksgiving

Maggie carefully executed her parallel parking in front of the row of old brownstones. *It's been years since I visited a neighborhood like this one. These places are amazing!* Fresh cut wreaths with shimmering red bows graced each door, ensconcing brass knockers.

She took a deep breath. *Come on, girl. You know you got this. Keep calm. You talk to complete strangers everyday about their felines and canines. You can certainly handle his parents.* She was still trying to wrap her mind around it. *He invited ME. He could have invited any of his other female friends, and heaven knows he's got his share of gorgeous ones, but he invited ME.*

Mags could confidently work a room full of people, no problem. She was sharp as a tack and sassy enough to turn heads while sparking uproarious laughter. But that was business. This was a very good-looking guy—a really rich, good-looking guy—and his stunningly influential family from the Mainline Philly region.

Her phone chirped. It was Alex telling her he'd pulled up and parked four cars back. His grandmother and grandfather were just arriving as well. "Perfect timing, Mags," Alex texted. "U get to meet my GRAND'S b4 the turkey's even carved. You should feel honored."

Now what is that supposed to mean? Is he serious or joking? Maggie wondered to herself. She still found Alex to be very much a puzzle—debonair, well educated, and oh-so-terribly serious—even bordering on pouty certain days. His nonverbal cues often projected that everyone owed him and his fine family some greater recognition. After all, how many present-day families could still boast of four generations of renowned architects graduating from the same Ivy-League university? Alex was the fourth in their lineage, and he made certain the right people regularly encountered this fact.

When he did try to be funny, it often came across rather pompous. Mags shrugged and chalked his most recent text up to such self-consumed perspective. *Ho-hum, cocky and dull,* she quietly assessed. *But wealthy, very wealthy,* she reminded herself. *A girl can probably put up with some doses of "dull and arrogant" for the right dollar.*

She stepped from her car, wrapped her argyle scarf tighter, and stepped onto the curb. Her knee-high, saddle-brown boots clomped against the cobblestone walkway as she moved toward Alex and his grandparents. Courteous hugs and quick quips of "What a pleasure to meet you!" were exchanged. Grandfather and grandmother were dressed to the nines, including elegant hats. The four made their way down the tree-lined walk and up the massive stone steps, seventh home on the right side in that block of Montgomery Avenue.

Stunning oak double doors with beveled and stained glass windows graced the front of the nineteenth century dwelling. Twelve-foot-high ceilings and pocket doors greeted them at the foyer, leading to the living room, complete with an original fireplace and carved mantle-piece. Alex's family's home was beautiful to behold, albeit there was something about it that conveyed the feel of a formidable fortress.

His parents greeted them at the door. The house was already bustling with extended family, the smell of delectable food, and the sound of seasonal music. Décor was point-on appropriate—an elegant blend of autumnal with a dash of almost-yuletide. *This has to be staged by one of Philly's finest interior designers.* Mags made a mental note.

She quickly learned from Alex's mother that although it was noontime, the full feast was still two to three hours from being served. *Oh no,* Maggie grimaced to herself. *This girl is starving.* Once deeper into the house, she was delighted to discover hors d'ocuvres, including the plumpest shrimp cocktail and the finest of fruit options, all artfully displayed around elegant centerpieces.

When Alex had invited her last Friday morning, he said there would be a few family and friends dropping by. "You could have warned me," she whispered as she grabbed another drink. "I had no clue that your folks know everyone who's anyone in Philadelphia." There was an impressive array of guests.

"Oh, this is only about half of the invite list," Alex shot back with a smug smile. "And we always have walk-ins, people who never bothered to RSVP. 'Annoys the heck out of my grandmother. It's glorious to watch."

Maggie courteously chuckled, but noted that she still didn't quite *get* Alex's offbeat comments. *Is this for real? Am I actually attending such an exquisite Thanksgiving celebration?* Mags was mentally pinching herself, in awe of her surroundings, the flavors, and the highbrow level of conversation. It was obvious that Alex and his family reveled in putting on airs.

Chitchat revealed that Alex's father held primary ownership of a large Mercedes-Benz dealership. Though his father had followed in the family footsteps with the architectural degree, "Real money, serious money started to flow once I broke from the bricks and mortar mold, to properly marry this family to Mercedes." Alex smiled big as his father rehearsed the history, while also leaning closer and putting his arm around Mags.

"I've made a lot of great decisions, Maggie, but rolling with Benz was my most brilliant ever, if I do say so." He went on to tell daring tales of cutthroat schemes. It had required shrewd maneuvering to mogul his way through the upper echelons of the Philly auto kingdoms and come out still standing.

As other more distant family members joined the circle, Alex's father began name-dropping, including the likes of Muhammad Ali, Donald Trump, and Kelly Ripa. Such names and stories were stated with that same serious, self-lauding tone that she had grown accustomed to hearing from Alex's voice. *Hmmm. Apple doesn't fall too far from the tree.* Mags readily saw the resemblance.

After dinner, coffee and tea were served. Alex's grandfather resumed the car business conversation, now touting the quality of Mercedes-Benz' seat leather when compared to the Japanese automakers' leather. All three generations of men were in solid agreement that Acura, Infiniti, and Lexus could never hold a candle to the deep-grain texture and thick stitch that went into a Benz. Maggie found herself spellbound by the luxury talk, yet also mildly put-off by the hoity-toity posture.

Hearing reference to the carmaker name Infiniti, her mind drifted toward Zach. Zach's daily drive was his G37. Sporting sleek lines, a jet-black body, and luxurious, tan leather seats, Mags knew what Zach would say. If he was here for the convo, he would now be embroiled in debate and vehemently taking on Alex. Maggie could not help but smile big with a mischievous grin.

She thought of her beloved Henry's bench seat. She'd spent many fall evenings shoulder to shoulder next to Zach, rolling down suburban lanes and even backcountry roads in Berks County. It was a down-to-earth blend of cloth and pleather, nostalgic 70s Naugahyde. She instinctively knew that Zach would argue for the genius of Ford's highly functional, no-frills design approach—only further evoking the pretentious posture of Alex's family.

Just then, Mags felt a tug on her sleeve. "Why not come join the more civilized conversation, dear," Grandmother coaxed with a warm grin. Maggie followed her to the dining room where she was quickly engulfed in voices of a half dozen Chatty Cathys.

One of Alex's aunts commenced, "I have insisted to Edward that we simply must take the family to St. Thomas during Christmas-New Year's week. Last year, we stayed home for the holidays. Every grandchild came to visit, and two or three of the darlings brought the influenza into our house. It was most dreadful, indeed."

"Well, Tony has already informed me," another aunt chimed, "there will be no exotic holiday travel for us this year. He's apparently shopped and dropped some very big bills on a handful of the rarest of gems." She had the circle's attention now. "Tony says he's gifting beautiful bling for his girls to wear now, but the kind of precious jewels which will be impressive investments to be passed down for generations to come." All ladies in the present-day Thanksgiving conversation were duly impressed. Mags politely smiled and nodded, attempting to fit in.

She stared back toward the living room, noting that several chairs near the fireplace were now clear of people. Drawn toward some silent space, the festive holly and ivy on the mantle, and the glow of the crackling flame, she found her way toward a tall oak rocker. She stared into the glowing embers and pondered. She could not help but wonder about Zach. *What might his family's Thanksgiving celebration feel like right now? I'm pretty confident it's a lot more down-to-earth than the discussions in this house.* Though she was personally moved by Alex's overtures, she found something to be deep-down disturbing about the family's level of self-absorption. *But then money can be marvelous, very marvelous.* She was self-coaching, as if she might convince herself.

Mags felt a tug on her sleeve. She turned to encounter a very short, elderly woman. "Hello there, young lady. You must be Maggie. You're here with Alex." Her greeting was warm. Her eyes gleamed with a depth of knowing, and Mags had that immediate, oh-so-strange sense, as if this tiny old woman was peering deep into her soul. "I'm Alex's great grandmother. Almost everyone calls me Noni. It's wonderful to meet you, Maggie!"

"It's a pleasure, actually a real delight, to meet you, Noni."

Their eyes locked as Noni's frail, bony fingers clasped Mags' hands.

"Beware the snare of all the flair. Remember, dear one, all that glitters is not truly so fair. Keep your heart open. More deeply care." Noni smiled big as she released Mags' hands, turned, and walked away. The wise old woman's rhythmic words arrested Maggie's thoughts. They felt otherworldly strange, yet captivating, and calming, all at the same time.

Just then, Alex stepped immediately in front of Maggie. With a suave and compelling smile, he extended his hand. "Come on, darling, there's a cousin I need you to meet." He said it with a want-to-show-you-off tone. Mags placed her hand in Alex's hand, and off they went.

CHAPTER 4

Xmas Trees and Bethlehem

"Who's up for dominoes?" Zach's cousin called across the house.

"Count me in!" Zach replied. *Maybe a little competition will spice things up.* Zach was hoping for his moping mood to improve. He was seriously missing Mags, no matter how hard he tried to not think about how her Thanksgiving might be unfolding. He had successfully resisted texting her all day. And she had strategically forgotten to tell him about her invitation to join Alex's family. Had he known, his mood would have been even more dismal.

Current crowd consensus at Gram's feast was to wait on pie and coffee. Everyone felt stuffed with turkey, rolls, and green bean casserole. Additional family and friends were yet to arrive, coming from other Thanksgiving gatherings around the county. Though loved ones would partake of big feasts from other places, it was tradition that everyone landed at Gram's in the evening for dessert, games, stories, and great laughter. Beyond Zach's family, additional close friends and neighbors always stopped by as well.

With Marshall's arrival just before sunset, Zach immediately marched him back out the door to examine Henry's tailgate and bumper. He had rehearsed the big Bubba tale for Gram when he arrived late the previous evening, but now he had to review the blow-by-blow for Marshall. The crisp November air provided Marshall with a chance for a puff on his pipe. Never smoking anything himself—Zach cringed at the health hazard—he actually enjoyed the sweet-smelling, second-hand savor of Marshall's pipe tobacco.

Ever the concerned mechanic, Marshall had to climb underneath to inspect. "Bumper still holdin' on good." He was pulling on the bolted areas. He stretched further and gave the exhaust pipes a tug. "Yep, lookin' tight. I'm thinkin' ya got off easy, well, 'cept those there rasc'ly scrapes and scuffs on his tailgate. Although I'd reckon some of those'll work out with a little scrubbin' and buffin' compound. How bad was the other fellers' truck?"

Zach gave a sinister chuckle. "You should have seen his front bumper. He's got much deeper gouges and some cracked grill pieces. His Chevy should have known better than to try chewing on a Ford. 'Got what he deserved, I'd say.'"

"So where's Miss Maggie?" Marshall couldn't resist asking. "Sure was nice havin' her 'round last summer. Looked like you two were gettin' 'long mighty fine." He grinned. "Guess she's prob'ly back in PA with her kin?"

"Yes, yes, she's with her family this weekend, at least I guess so." Zach rolled his eyes and shrugged, as if to give the vague impression he might not really care.

Marshall stared a knowing look and puffed on his pipe. "Trouble in paradise, eh?"

"Oh, I guess you could say that. Everything seemed fantastic between us, all across the rest of summer and then into fall. I honestly thought our relationship was going somewhere very significant, maybe even toward our getting engaged sometime soon."

"Hmm, that serious, eh?" Marshall was listening intently and nodding as Zach was opening up. They both leaned against Henry's bed.

"Yes, but then last Friday," Zach continued, "Well, I don't know what I said or did, but she started acting strange. And the beginning of the week, before leaving to come this way, everything was off-beat between us, like something had shifted in her view of me."

"Hey, guys! Come and get it! Pie and coffee are ready, out on the counter!" Gram was calling from the side door of the house.

"Okay, we're coming. Thanks, Gram!"

"We better head back in and join 'em," Marshall replied, "But what are you doin' tomorrow? I got piles of firewood out by the garage, needs a splittin'. How 'bout you stop down for a spell? We can split wood and talk more."

"I can do that," Zach shot back. "And it's the perfect excuse for me to get out of having to go Black Friday shopping. Thanks, Marsh'. You're a real deliverer!"

"Glad to help a fella in need," Marshall said, laughing.

Back inside, Gram's kitchen and living room were now abuzz with the cousins, aunts, and uncles enjoying various board games, sundry pies, tea, and coffee. Zach found the dominoes table and joined the circle of competitors. Apparently, the fresh air and his opportunity to vent a bit with Marshall had done his head some good, clearing the clouds of confusion, at least a bit.

He successfully settled into fun play, scrumptious pie, and laughter. He was winning at dominoes, and Zach loved to win. All was rolling well for an hour or so when suddenly, Zach thought he heard a familiar voice come through the kitchen door.

"HELLO! Thanksgiving blessings to all of you! The good Lord certainly has blessed us abundantly—real good, all the time. And we have every reason to be thankful, one and all!" The voice was deep and booming.

Oh no! Zach was quickly realizing. *It's Uncle Clyde! Is there any hope of my being delivered from the rest of this evening?* He seriously looked for the nearest exit.

Clyde was Zach's larger-than-life, boisterous, preacher-uncle. He had pastored a flock of folks tucked in the middle of nowheresville in south-central Ohio for many years. Though the church's heyday had come and gone, "Brother Clyde" was still well known by people across the region. While others might appreciate his brash style of sharing, Zach found him to be pretentious and rather pesky with his frequent spouting of Christian platitudes. *I'll just stay focused on dominoes and pie. Try to act like I don't know he's arrived.*

Within a few minutes, Uncle Clyde found his way toward Zach and the other domino players. With a general greeting to everyone, he pulled up a seat and invaded the game.

"How are you, Zachary?!" Uncle Clyde now seemed oblivious to the other cousins. *Why does he have to pay so much attention to ME?* Zach wondered to himself. *What did I ever do to deserve such a privileged-nephew status?* The cousins took this as their cue to go refresh coffee and slice second pieces of pie.

"I'm doing well, doing well, Uncle Clyde." Zach was working to be courteous as he braced for the inevitable onslaught of uncomfortable inquisition.

"So how is that little architectural work of yours?" Zach could not help but cringe. His uncle held a personal preoccupation for all things ultra-spiritualized, including a great penchant for everything churchy. He specialized in downplaying other people's vocational pursuits and up-playing his own ministry endeavors. For Uncle Clyde, serving the Lord in church work was the truest and noblest of callings.

"Overall, the firm is doing pretty well. We still have our daily challenges of big projects, pushy clients, and financial pressures, especially in seasons like right now." Zach's voice gave him away. He was nervous and more than a little scared.

Uncle Clyde jumped at what he saw as the teachable moment. "Well, Zachary, it's all-too-easy for money-hungry businesses—not just yours, mind you, but corporate types everywhere—to forget what makes this time of year truly meaningful. Never forget, Jesus is the reason for the season. We must keep Christ in Christmas!" It was said with his best preacher-ish passion.

Zach just stared back and bit his tongue. This was the very kind of platitudinous theologizing that evoked Zach's deep-inside eye rolling and overall dislike of his uncle. Brother Clyde proceeded to rehearse the tragedy of one local Christmas tree sales stand that no longer stated "Christmas Trees for Sale." All of their signs proclaimed: "Xmas Trees for Sale." Zach was profusely rolling his internal eyes with great disgust, and reacting more than ever. *Is Xmas versus Christmas actually a battle worth fighting?*

"You know, Zach," Uncle Clyde added with quieter reflection, "I think what you need is a good trip back to Bethlehem!"

"What in the world do you mean by *that*?" Zach audibly queried, complete with more than a twinge of unmasked cynicism.

"Okay, hear me out now, Son!" Zach winced inside. *I'm not his son. Why does he have to make such belittling references? Good golly, I'm headed toward thirty years old.*

"When is the last time you actually paid a visit to those original characters of Christmas?" Zach was still giving him an incredulous look. "I'm not talking a literal visit. How about exploring them again—what they do and what they say—on the dusty pages of the Good Book's original Christmas story?"

Zach was ready to interject, but Brother Clyde was on a roll.

"Truth is, they were just common folk, working hard in the everyday rough and tumble of life. Joseph was a carpenter. Mary was most likely from a farming family. The shepherds were working the night shift in the fields. But they all started to personally encounter God's work in their own lives. How those different characters responded to actually work with God reveals faith-filled courage, anticipation of kingdom mission, a choice to rejoice, and remarkable levels of others-oriented, gracious generosity."

Zach was suddenly speechless. These words had to express some of the most profound concepts he had ever heard roll off his uncle's lips.

"Well, okay, um, yes, 'Appreciate that input, Uncle Clyde." Zach's response conveyed a mix of sincere gratitude blended with hesitant caution. Saying too much might evoke a full-fledged, forty-five minute sermon, complete with exposition of each correlating biblical passage.

Uncle Clyde gave a genuine smile. "Try it, Zachary. I dare you. Give Mary and Joseph, the angels, shepherds, wise men—even some of the lesser-known supporting cast members—some deeper thought this season. I think you'll be a bit surprised. What you discover might be life-changing, even for your business. Well, I better let you and your cousins get back to dominoes."

As his uncle moved to the other side of the room, Zach moved to the kitchen to slice his second piece of pie. As he did, he was pondering. *Could he be right? Might there be something even more significant to discover this Christmas about God's work through the characters and events of Christmas?*

Zach shook his head, thinking deeply. *What did Uncle Clyde say?* He was working to recall what he said he might discover. *Let's see. I know he mentioned faith-filled courage. God knows I need a bunch of that right now.* He cut into the pecan pie and poured more coffee.

CHAPTER 5

Choppin' Wood and Christmas Quotes

Friday morning, Henry hummed his low-pitch, grumble-rumble as Zach steered his way back the lane to Marshall's house. The old F100's engine purred. Plugs had been changed last summer. Timing had been adjusted, and his carburetor was rebuilt. Though his joints were still moving strong, the old fella's body shook, rattled, and squeaked at points—sure signs of some automotive arthritis setting in.

"Mornin', Zach!" Marshall was already swinging his ax near a tall pile of logs. "How'd the evenin' wrap up? Looked like you an' cuzins were havin' one mean game o' dominoes."

"Oh, we managed. Nobody suffers too much when Gram's pies are involved."

Marshall swung strong, letting his ax's head embed in a thick chunk of oak. He rested his foot atop the log and took a bright red handkerchief from his overalls. Mopping his brow, he gulped fresh iced tea from his old green metal thermos. Temperatures were above normal for late November in Ohio, with some drizzly rain forecast for later in the day. Chopping wood was vigorous, so it was easy to work up a strong thirst and ample sweat even on Thanksgiving weekend.

Zach began retrieving and stacking the pieces Marsh' had already split. He could not help but wish it would snow. *Some flakes in the air would make it feel more Christmassy. 'Always seems like the final days of November in Ohio are so dull and gray.*

"What's a chewin' at you?" Apparently, Marshall could read Zach's generally deplorable disposition. "Sure seems like there's more to it than just missin' Maggie. Go 'head. Git it off your chest."

Zach grinned and shook his head at Marshall's way of skipping the pleasantries, no beating around the bush. He liked such a no-nonsense, get-to-the-point approach.

"Well, when I left here last summer after Grandpa went to glory, I was so motivated to live out my faith everyday, to do all my workday tasks for God's glory. I really wanted to go back to the firm, ready to be a workplace missionary. I was revved up to love and serve other people, to help them meet Christ, and to come into his kingdom."

Marshall interjected. "You did leave here pretty fired up, as I 'member it. Mags too. But let me guess. It wasn't so easy?"

"EXACTLY!" Zach seemed amazed, like Marshall might be psychic.

"First couple days back at the firm seemed fantastic. My task list seemed VERY purposeful. Interactions with people were so alive with potential. But very soon—just a few days, really—my pace felt frazzled and hectic again, and before I knew it, the same old problems emerged with rascally clients and coworkers."

Marshall was listening close, nodding, and repacking his pipe. "I truly tried, Marsh—*seriously* tried to show Christ's love. I sensed some good potential was developing. Some of our team started to actually recognize Christ through me. I had a couple solid conversations about faith-related issues— several people were opening up—but then the *new guy* arrived." Zach said it with disgust.

"New guy?" Marshall queried curiously.

"Yes. Alex." Zach spit out the name like he had just tasted something rotten.

"He thinks he's high and mighty. 'Comes from some influential Philly family, apparently wicked wealthy. Maggie's dad hired him based on a strong portfolio and some big-name references. They all promised that he showed great potential. First opportunity in early fall, he introduced a couple new era, glass curtain walls into one of our big project's plans. The whole team went crazy with cheers when they saw it. I was thinking, what's the big deal with glass? Anybody can drop in glass curtains. He's a one-trick pony, if you ask me."

Marshall started chuckling. "Squirmin' a little, Zach. Yer uncomfortable with another cook in the kitchen. 'Least that's what I'm thinkin', if you're askin' me." Marshall grinned as he puffed and blew a splendid smoke ring toward the barn. His big eyes seemed to pierce right through Zach's jealous soul.

Wrinkling his nose and running his hands back through his thick curls, Zach chose to change the subject. "I've got to admit, Marsh, I'm really not feeling like it's the holidays. I tried listening to Christmas tunes on the trek here the other night. Every other song that played had love lyrics and made me think of Maggie. I rolled into Belleville, and Bubba and Godzilla chomped on Henry's tail. Then last night at Gram's, Uncle Clyde came along with his jolly Christmas quotes."

"What Christmas quotes?" Marshall wondered.

"You know, his typical, way-too-cheesy ones. *Keep Christ in Christmas. Jesus is the reason for the season.*" Zach let them roll off his tongue with his best sarcasm. "I know they're true. I get the point. But, well—"

Zach settled now, speaking with a more thoughtful, pensive tone. "Really, I do grasp it. But Uncle Clyde said these words as if I need to be converted to believe in Christmas. He even insinuated these truths might help my business and workplace perspective."

"What if your preacher-uncle is right?" Marshall shot back.

Zach stared at him in disbelief, as if to say, *Hey, I thought you'd be on my side!*

"Jus' encouragin' you to slow down a bit." Marshall paused. He could tell Zach was bothered. "Quit jumpin' and rushin' bout everything. Maybe Miss Maggie is just needin' some time to sort out what she's feelin' bout you. And there's a good chance there's sumpin' more to Alex than you're thinkin'. And maybe God's been workin' bunches 'cross the years through ye ole' holy family. You know, Mar' and Joe, the Angel Gabe and those wise guys."

Zach startled chuckling aloud. He frequently found Marshall's lingo to be laughable, but he usually contained his humor. This time, there was no containing it. *Who calls them Mar' and Joe—only Marshall.* Zach mused to himself and laughed some more.

"Now you're really sounding like my uncle. He told me I should revisit those same characters of Christmas. I'm sensing a theme." They both grinned.

Marshall picked up his ax and went back to chopping wood. Zach resumed stacking. "The fascinating thing, Marsh', is that Uncle Clyde moved off his pithy little quotes and said something so thoughtful. It grabbed me—so provocative that I captured it right before I went to sleep last night."

Zack stacked his armful of logs on the pile, took off his gloves, and retrieved his phone from his pocket. Tapping on his Notes app, he read what he'd entered the previous night: "Journey back to Bethlehem this Christmas to discover what the characters teach me about faith-filled courage, kingdom anticipation, a choice to rejoice, and gracious generosity."

"Well, that's a mighty tall order for one Christmas, I'd say."

"Yes, Marsh', yes it is. But I'm sensing I need to chase this." Zach wrinkled his nose and ran his hands through his hair again. "I've got no clue where it's all going."

He put his gloves back on his hands. Just then, his phone chirped. Zach grabbed his phone. It was a text—Zach's heart skipped five beats—it was from Mags.

CHAPTER 6

Stitches and Courageous Texts

There was no resisting. He had to take his gloves back off in order to read the text from Maggie. "I'll be right back, Marshall. 'Need my iced tea from the truck." Zach was trying to play it cool and not have to explain why he was jumping to check a message.

While retrieving his tea, he tapped on Mags' message: "Hope you're having a good weekend at Gram's. I'm shopping with my mom. When you're back, we need to talk."

"That's IT?" Zach said it aloud in disbelief. Her text felt cryptic and cold. "What in the world am I supposed to make of that?" *It says nothing and seems foreboding.*

"OUCCHHHHH! AHHHHH!" Marshall was suddenly howling.

Zach dropped his phone on Henry's seat and ran toward the woodpile. Marsh' was on the ground, grabbing both his ankle and his head. There was blood. Zach rushed to him and dropped to the ground.

"Are you okay? What's wrong? What happened?"

"Not tot'ly sure." Marshall was grimacing as he swiped blood from his brow. Zach was relieved. Marshall was able to speak as he sat up. "I think I stepped wrong. Must've stepped on that log, turnin' my ankle and tumblin' over. Ax went a flyin', and my head caught it on the way down.

"Let me see that," Zach said with a fatherly tone. He pulled back the red handkerchief that Marshall had instinctively pulled from his bibs. "Ouch is an understatement, Marsh'. That's a deep gouge, very deep."

"Oh, can't be that bad." Marsh was quickly trying to gather his wits about him. He tried to stand. As he did, he almost toppled again as he tried to put weight on his foot. He looked like a Weeble wobbling but about to fall down. Zach caught him.

"Okay, come on, my friend. Let's roll to the ER."

"Nooo! No, sir! Can't be that bad. I hate goin' to docs, and we'll be awaitin' forever in an emergency room." Marshall was speaking, but his voice conveyed a greater sense of strain and agony now. "I could prob'ly stitch 'er up myself."

"No way, and no more arguing!" Zach insisted as he wrapped Marshall's arm over his head and around his shoulder. They hobbled their way toward Henry.

Once they arrived at the hospital, the ER was less packed than usual, and Marshall's wait was relatively short. They were soon ushered behind a curtained evaluation room where a nurse performed the normal preliminaries. The bleeding had slowed, and now they were just waiting to see the doctor. Marshall seemed stable.

"Are you okay for a minute?" Zach asked Marshall. "Mind if I step out for just a couple moments?" Marshall nodded a reassuring "No problem."

Zach tapped his phone keys to send a text to Doc Ben. The oh-so-wise, kind sage Benjamin Clinton was his grandfather's long time friend, previously a university professor now part-time chaplain at the hospital.

"Hey, Doc! Happen to be here at the hospital? Marshall and I are in the ER. I think he's okay. Took a tumble while chopping wood."

Within moments, Doc responded: "I'm not on-site right now. Keep me posted on his condition. Will U B @church 2morrow?"

"Yes," Zach tapped back. "Not leaving for PA until afternoon."

"Great! Want to meet for coffee b4 service?"

"That'd be wonderful. Church café?" Zach asked.

"Yup. Looking forward to catching up! How bout 8am?"

Zach checked back on Marshall. The doctor had verified a sprained ankle, prescribed some pain meds, and he was placing several stitches in Marsh's wrinkled forehead. Within the hour they were on their way home.

After getting Marshall settled back at home and tidying up the woodpiles, Zach rolled back to Gram's. Last of the visiting family members were loading vehicles to head home. Zach would be the only one to spend one more night before heading back to Valley Forge on Sunday afternoon.

Everyone was relieved to learn that Marshall was home, on the mend, and resting. The final cars pulled out the drive, and Gram smiled like she was hatching a plan.

"Well, Zachary, it's just you and me. It's Black Friday. Leftover turkey and stuffing was already the spread here over lunch. I'm sick of cooking. I'd say it's a pizza night."

"Sounds like a scrumptious plan, Gram!"

They settled in at their favorite, the Pizza Cottage. Their order was one large pizza, half hamburger and onion, the other half pepperoni, plus two large Pepsis.

"Heard anything from Mags?" Gram asked cautiously as their drinks arrived.

"In fact, I did," Zach replied, "But I'm not certain what to make of it." He rehearsed why and rolled his eyes. "Just adds to how complex and jumbled everything feels right now. It's supposed to be the most wonderful time of the year. What a crock! Seems to me it's more like the most wretched time of the year."

Gram chuckled. "Now, now, Zachary, you can't really mean that. If you do, there must be more eating at you than just Mags' being a bit distant."

Zach proceeded to rehearse his frustrations back at work, his financial fears, and overall gloomy perspective. He also reviewed Uncle Clyde's nudging for him to journey back to Bethlehem, to rediscover the Christmas characters.

"And you know what's even worse, Gram? Marshall had the audacity to agree with Uncle Clyde, like he was on his side! 'Said I should take it seriously." Zach paused. "Okay, I mean, there's probably *something* to gain, but I just don't know what to think right now."

"Well," Gram grinned as the pizza arrived, "I'd say there's *a lot* to gain. It sounds to me like you need a fresh dose of Christmas courage, a fresh sense of adventure, like the original characters."

Zach gave her a puzzled look as he chomped on a slice of pepperoni.

"Yes, have you considered it? God appeared to Joseph, who was in the royal family line of the famous King David. Joseph was a carpenter, engaged to young Mary. The angel appeared to Joseph, and the first thing he said was, 'Don't be afraid!' And then he explained that Mary was expecting a baby, conceived by the Holy Spirit. Can you imagine what it took for Joseph to actually buy that?"

"Yea, that *would* be some big news to receive and really believe." Zach shook his head.

"And the angel told him to go ahead, move forward with marrying her, because this child would be the deliverer, the savior for people. Think about it. God was calling Joseph to take a risk, go ahead, even though it would most certainly mean ridicule. God was urging Joseph to break from the norm—really go out on a limb. Most of us humans make big life decisions based on our fears. Instead, God was urging Joseph to lead his life and others' lives based on faith."

"So that's the faith-filled courage Uncle Clyde was talking about?" Zach's face sported that look of fresh discovery.

"Yes, God was stretching him outside his comfort zone, that's for sure. And it seems he's still calling people toward that today. He urges us to take holy risks in our business ventures, in new avenues of mission, and even daring new steps with those we claim we love. We dare not forget that God's work in the first Christmas story involved a love story. That holy couple of Christmas, well, Mary and Joseph were very much two young love birds."

"Are you saying what I think you're saying?" Zach asked with some blushing curiosity. "Is there some kind of courage I need to take in my relationship with Mags?"

"Maybe so. Maybe so, Zach, but it may also be that it's time to step into some faith-filled adventures in other areas as well. Perhaps you've given up too quickly regarding making an impact for Christ with others through your daily work.

Perhaps God has some unique way he wants you to join his work this Christmas." Gram was expressing this with a twinkle of spry anticipation in her eyes.

They paid their tab and reveled in the glory of the post-Thanksgiving feast. Pizza and Pepsi were one of their favorite combinations. "So good to the taste buds!" Zach exclaimed.

Back home, they continued their conversation about Joseph and faith-filled courage. Gram suddenly gained her own whimsical look. "Say, Zachary, I just recalled something that fits all of this, and it's stunningly appropriate to all we are discussing."

"What's that, Gram?"

She headed for her library bookshelves, retrieved a favorite, and returned to the kitchen table. "Listen to these stirring words by C.S. Lewis." Gram flicked pages with her fingers, making her way to a familiar set of lines.

"Make your choice, adventurous stranger. Strike the bell and bide the danger, or wonder till it drives you mad, what would have followed if you had."

"Wow, read that again, please." Zach was stirred. "I've heard and read a lot of Lewis—but never that one."

Gram repeated the soul-echoing lines slowly. As he listened, he could not help but remember the look on that sculptured face, Joseph's snow-dusted visage on Wednesday evening outside the old brick church. He had been moved by his look of courageous resolve.

Before he went to sleep, Zach glanced again at his text from Mags. *How in the world do I reply to this?* Even as the question haunted his thoughts, he could hear the angel's words to Joseph once again. "Do not be afraid to—"

Choosing a fresh batch of faith-filled courage, Zach hit reply: "Hi Mags! Having an adventuresome time at Gram's— great food and intriguing conversations. Much to share when I'm back, including a few things I've wanted to say to you for a while. Up 'til now I was scared."

Suddenly, Zach paused—he was second-guessing—and he started ferociously deleting. He stopped, took a deep breath, and remembered God's work in Joseph that first Christmas. *Joseph responded to the angel's words with faith-filled courage. I really can do the same.* Zach started retyping those same bold words of self-revelation. Then with one bold stroke, he hit "Send." There it went.

He then realized he'd failed to tell her about Henry's newest injury from the gobbling Godzilla truck. Within moments, he had a message back from Mags. "So sorry to hear about Henry's hurting tailgate. Are you okay?"

Thus began a volley of texts, but the final one from Mags simply said, "Looking forward to catching up together on Monday! Hugs. Good night!" And with that text, Zach found his heart beating faster. He was oh-so-glad he'd been courageous.

Advent Week 1: Reflections and Exercises
on Faith-Filled Courage

1. What's your favorite memory from past Christmastimes? (perhaps a day of shopping or feasting with family and friends) Share the details.

2. Can you relate with Zach and Mags' personal frustrations thus far in the story? Describe your own fears and struggles during this current season.

3. Do you anticipate this year's season will be relatively tranquil or ridiculously stressful? Why?

4. Read Matthew 1:18–25. What do you find most stunning about the angel's words to Joseph? How might you have felt if you were Joseph?

5. If you contemplate the collection of characters in the nativity scene, with which of them can you most readily identify? Why?

6. How does the tone at Zach's gram's house compare and contrast with the overall atmosphere at Alex's house?

7. When and where have you encountered Uncle Clyde's seasonal mantras: "Jesus is the reason for the season," and "Keep Christ in Christmas?" Are you comforted or bothered by such statements? Why?

8. How are you encouraged by the C.S. Lewis quotation? Is there an arena of your life where you need to heed Lewis' words and the angel's urging?

9. Watch the Christmas film, *The Nativity Story: The Journey of a Lifetime, a Story for All Time.* View it together as a family or with a group of friends. Discuss what stirred in you as you watched and which character(s) was most compelling. Why?

10. If you have not already, decorate a nativity crèche with your family or a group of friends. As you do, discuss the characters and how you might resonate.

ADVENT WEEK 2: DISCOVERING KINGDOM ANTICIPATION

CHAPTER 7

Coffee and Kingly Incarnation

Espresso machines were just warming up when Zach arrived a few minutes before eight o'clock. Doc Ben was already there, but he was the only person inhabiting the place, other than café workers. First service didn't start until nine, which meant they'd have almost an hour before the invasion began in earnest. People at this church loved engaging in worship that was fully caffeinated.

Doc was sporting a well-worn, comfy-brown, corduroy jacket. His leather bag was slung over a chair back, and his journal was flopped open. He had been busy capturing thoughts and nursing a rich, frothy concoction of some sort. Zach surmised it was likely some incarnation of cappuccino.

"So what's happening these days?" Ben asked with a jump-right-in tone.

"Well, a whole bunch, really." Zach set down his coffee and ran his fingers through his thick curls. Letting it all pour out, he began rehearsing the sundry highlights. He shared his frustration over his less-than-productive attempts to share Christ's love with others in his workplace, his fears over this seasonal financial crunch, and then his relational woes with Mags. He made certain, though, to tell Doc about his burst of courage the previous evening and the potentially positive glimmer of hope from Maggie's final blast of texts.

Doc Ben was smiling big and soaking up his every word. It felt like Zach's heartfelt, lengthy explanation might be wrapping up, so Doc jumped in. "It sounds like you're wrestling with deeply profound and very normal issues, at least for leaders like you who actually dare to make progress on their adventures."

Zach's face reflected a look of calmer, affirmed relief.

"And whether you like to hear it or not, 'sounds like you're getting solid feedback from Uncle Clyde."

"Oh, GREAT! Thanks a lot." Zach was rolling his eyes and wrinkling his nose. "You're joining the applauding throng of supporters. Marshall seemed to love my uncle's comments—Gram as well."

"Okay, but let me feed your cynical hunger for something even more substantive, at least just a bit, because there really is some more food for thought on this." Doc had a sparkle of insight in his eyes.

"Excellent!" Zach leaned in with intrigue as he took another sip of coffee. "I'm ready for a big helping of something next-level to chew on—something more than *Keep Christ in Christmas* and *Jesus is the reason for the season.*"

"I'm surprised he didn't bring up the battle of *Merry Christmas versus Happy Holidays.*" Doc chuckled at his own wit.

"Actually, Uncle Clyde *did* spotlight the evils of selling *Xmas* trees," Zach volleyed. "Poor tree sales guy wouldn't have had a chance selling Charlie Brown's pathetic tree to my uncle on *that* particular evening."

"Truth is, Zachary, your questions and frustrations could not have culminated in a brighter season. Christmas, this entire time of Advent, is really all about God's fresh work, both his initiative and his calling of humans into a new chapter for our own daily work. As Christ arrived, he came to earth as 'God incarnate.' That's a rather sophisticated way that scholars speak of the Divine One actually revealing himself in human form here on earth."

"God in a human body," Zach added, nodding and affirming his own grasp of the idea.

"Yes, the Gospel of John, chapter one supplies intriguing explanation of this. John tells us that in Christ's arrival, God 'tented' or set himself up like a 'tabernacle among us.' What we often skip over is John's very poetic connections—his deliberate choice of words—brilliantly mirroring Genesis' opening lines, the opening sections of God's story. He uses words like 'in the beginning' and 'light.' But there's something stunning we've too typically skipped over."

Zach looked intrigued. Many more early service congregants were now starting to populate the café. The wondrous aroma of mochas and fresh muffins was now filling the air. However, Doc Ben's lowered voice and captivating thoughts had Zach so transfixed he barely realized so many others were present.

"As God's people, the Israelites had wandered in the wilderness those hundreds of years ago. God's glory was among them, his holy presence above the Ark of the Covenant in the tabernacle. This was their constant reminder that their glorious King was in their midst. This was the same King of Creation, as revealed in Genesis 1 and 2."

"Whoa, wait a minute!" Zach's voice carried that excited edge of discovery. "So the Gospel writer, John, is telling us that in Jesus' coming, the King has arrived among us. He's here, in a body. The King is tenting among us."

"You're putting the pieces together, Zach. Very good. How about refills?"

They stood and headed for the café counter. "And I'm guessing there's even more to discover, right?" Zach grinned as he awaited his next cup. He had learned that Doc's insights were almost endless.

CHAPTER 8

Christmas at Work

Their mugs were refreshed with piping hot coffee. Doc Ben was smiling as they sat back down. "Yes, but there's more to this than just Apostle John's emphasis that the King has arrived. You mentioned your personal motivation toward courage, based on Joseph's example. That story comes our way in Matthew, chapter 1. And it's important to remember that Saint Matthew's big goal, his driving aim, was to show us Jesus as the promised Messiah-King. We commonly get that concept *mostly* right at Christmas, recognizing his kingship, especially when we sing certain songs. I'm thinking of portions from Handel's *Messiah*.

"Lines like 'HE shall reign, forever and EVER.'" Zach sang it with some real bravado. He was following Doc's thread with great precision.

Doc chuckled. "Yes, but what we commonly miss is the fuller sense of *what* the King came to accomplish." There was a pregnant pause and a couple silent beats.

Zach sported a "Duh, Captain Obvious" look, though he did not vocalize it.

Ben knew exactly what he was thinking. "People quickly assume his incarnation's purpose was to come to earth, to die on the cross, to forgive our sins, and take us to heaven someday."

"Right on, Doc. Exactly! He came to bring God's eternal love." Zach was nodding as he said it with a self-congratulating tone. He was quite confident he had the correct answer. "And this brings an eternal perspective to Christmas. God's love came down for us at Christmastime. It's beautiful!"

"Yes, that's all true. But hold your horses. That's really only part of the story, Zachary."

Now Zach was puzzled all the more. He had learned that Doc usually had a next-level, deeper concept to share when he addressed him as Zachary. It was apparently a throwback to his classroom days at the university, calling on students with their fuller names during question and answer time.

"The King's arrival and role meant so much more. You may recall that humans were made in the image of God, according to that opening scene in Genesis. A big part of the first man and woman's calling included God's charge 'to rule and to reign,' to be 'kings and queens' over the creation."

"I'm remembering pieces of this from our conversation last summer," Zach responded with excitement.

"Genesis 2, verse fifteen relates God's unique purpose for the man to work to cultivate the garden, but by Genesis 3, everything turns topsy-turvy. Humans chose to eat the fruit, thus rebelling and disobeying their Creator-King. The resulting curse included debilitating effects on all of creation, and sadly enough, such cursed conditions included our work. One of the very big, ugly outcomes of humanity's fall was how mixed up, messed up, and frustrating our daily work became. We now have to scratch out an existence by the sweat of our brows. We readily find ourselves struggling to thrive, often short-circuited emotionally, and even frustrated relationally in our daily labors."

"Sounds like most of my daily existence," Zach shot back with a cynical snicker. "No, seriously, I'm recalling that this is all part of what God set out to graciously redeem."

"Yes, exactly right!" Doc Ben affirmed with enthusiasm. "And since his arrival here on earth, King Jesus has been actively working out such redemptive plans. We can sincerely hold great kingdom anticipation during the Christmas season. The King has arrived, and the scope of his work means that our labors can be—and most definitely *should be*— infused with his kingdom mission."

Zach had a puzzled, questioning look on his face. "So let me get this straight. Many, many days, my job's tasks and conversations still feel exhausting, utterly frustrating in fact. But Jesus' arrival can help my outlook and outcomes?" Zach was synthesizing his own conclusion, even as he asked the deeper question.

"Right on!" Doc was enthused at Zach's correlations. "You got it, and here's why. As we celebrate Christmas, we revisit Christ's coming. His purpose was to reverse the ugly curse, including the horrific results that show up in our daily work endeavors. So while we still face the sweat, the frustrations, and overall agony of our still-imperfect work experiences, we can regroup and rejoice. We can find greater hope, confidence, and endurance through knowing that Christ has come. He is working better things with stronger effects through his long-term plans."

"It also hits me," Zach chimed in, "that Christ's own work here on earth was tangible, both early on as a carpenter and then later with his hands-on approach. He was very committed to seriously helping and healing people."

"Yes, yes indeed!" Doc was agreeing with enthusiasm. "Mark 6:3. People were amazed, wondering where he got his wisdom. They readily recognized him as 'the carpenter.' He knew the rough and tumble of everyday ordinary hard work. His family business was a big part of his incarnation as well."

Zach tipped his head inquisitively. "Seems that if his coming at Christmas included his aim to redeem our work, then we should deliberately choose better attitudes, find fresh motivation to do even stronger work, and aim to be even more creative in our plans to accomplish greater things."

"There you go, Zachary. I'd dare to say you can dream, scheme, and otherwise plan for the best buildings ever designed. And what if frustrated medical researchers let the aim of Christmas motivate them to keep pursuing better medical breakthroughs? And what if automotive repair professionals were to leverage the season to envision new ways of improving and expanding their car care and customer service as they move into the New Year?"

Zach was nodding. "Seems like this should be the most wonderful time of the year for more reasons than the shopping, feasting, and potential for snowfall. Of course, heaven only knows if we'll see any of the white stuff this year." He said it with his typical level of snarky pessimism.

Suddenly, they both jolted back to actual space-time continuum. The sound of music was rushing into the café. The worship gathering was just moments from starting. But a glance at the big clock revealed something stunning. It was indeed time for the service to start. *Second* service. They had passionately talked for over two hours.

"Hey, Zach, good to see you again!" It was a familiar face and friendly tone, and then a big handshake.

Zach was struggling to come up with his name. "Yea, uh, good to see *you* too."

"Hope you haven't forgotten about Haiti, man." Suddenly, Zach was remembering. It was James, one of the church's Haiti team members.

"The crew here is working to put together another trip, probably next February or March. We'll be doing some community planning and construction skills training. You should go."

Before Zach could say "yay" or "nay," James was handing him his business card.

"Call me. I'll give you the scoop on what we're scheming. I've gotta join my family in the service. Give me a shout."

"Okay. Big thanks, James. Will do."

As Zach and Doc placed their coffee mugs on the café counter, Zach started chuckling. "You realize what we just talked about—what's at the core of those ideas we teased out together, don't you?"

Now Doc Ben was sporting an uncharacteristic look of puzzlement.

Zach laughed at his own realization. "The second characteristic Uncle Clyde said I'd discover if I revisited Bethlehem. *Kingdom anticipation.* We were just talking about the King's arrival and the renewal of royal purposes for our daily work—for his kingdom to more fully come here on earth, his mission to gain momentum in the here and now."

He was shaking his head. "Amazing. Gram and I ended up talking about *faith-filled courage.* How did my uncle *know* we'd talk about such things?"

Doc started grinning the broadest smile. "Looks like you better keep your eyes and ears wide open. You've obviously embarked on the adventure, ready or not."

"That's for sure," Zach affirmed. "I just hope this afternoon's journey back to Pennsylvania proves to be safe, smooth travels for Henry. Our road trip here held more than enough adventure for one holiday season!"

CHAPTER 9

Quoting Angels

A quick flip of the switch illuminated so much more than the normal office lights. "Wow!" Zach exclaimed aloud. "That's bright!"

He was the first to roll into the office at Brinkley Design-Build on the Monday morning after Thanksgiving. It was about 7:30. Zach was not expecting the explosion of Christmas brilliance that greeted him as he turned on the office lights. *Elves must have snuck in and done some decorating during the weekend.* Zack chuckled and thought how much the seasonal décor betrayed Mags' handiwork. The glowing blast of lights effectively spread good Christmas cheer, even drawing out a smile from Zachary's all-too-typically glum, post-holiday-weekend disposition.

Zach dropped his bag in his office and headed to the staff kitchen to start some coffee brewing. Within a few minutes, he heard footsteps and the jingle of keys.

"Good morning, Zach! Welcome back." Larry's voice echoed down the hall. Although he hadn't actually seen Zach, he had surmised his office door was already open, with light emanating into the dark corridor.

"Hello, Larry. How are you? How were the Brinkley festivities?" Zach asked with honest interest, though he felt some sudden waves of awkwardness. He hadn't counted on being alone early morning at the office with Mags' dad. *Does he know that things have been off-kilter between Mags and me? Could he have sensed that I've felt frustrated and fearful about work, our current financial condition, and my work in general? I wonder if he's on to me.*

"We had a splendid Thanksgiving weekend, Zach!" Larry was more chipper, positive, and enthusiastic than usual. *Man, maybe he should take a holiday more often.* Zach was curious over Larry's out-of-character, extra-good mood.

"It was actually rather quiet on Thanksgiving Day at our place. Only a few family members dropped in for the meal— and just a bunch of us old-timers at that. Of course, Mags was gone, and—"

Larry continued babbling about their meal and conversation, but nothing else he said was actually registering for Zachary. He was stuck on "Mags was gone." *Where? With whom? Why? And why didn't I know this?*

"Say, I'm calling an all-hands-on-deck meeting." This abruptly retrieved Zach's attention. "My office, 9.30 sharp. I'll shoot an e-mail, but make sure everybody knows."

"Okay," Zach responded cautiously. "Anything to prep for? Everything okay?" His boss's sudden call for a meeting put Zach's nerves on high alert. He wondered if he might coax some advance explanation out of him.

"Oh, yes, *all good*." Larry gave a big smile. "That's what the meeting is about! I have some very good news. I'll share the full scoop when everyone gathers, but I'm rather optimistic that it holds the potential for setting an amazing tone for our December as a firm!"

He had Zach's full attention now. "Are you serious—a new killer project? Something big?" His voice was exuding curious enthusiasm.

"Yes. It holds great promise ... well, sort of." Larry suddenly pulled his cards back closer to his chest. He grinned, almost mischievous. "I'll just say it's *good news of great joy, which shall be for all the people*."

Zack laughed. "Wow. This *must* be good if you're quoting angels." He felt some healthy pride that he recognized those words from the Luke 2 story. There were shepherds, angels, and blinding, bright-light glory in the fields that night. His synapses were firing with rapid recollection. As a fifth grader, Zach had worn a bathrobe, carried a crooked stick, and quoted the section from memory, word for word in the church Christmas pageant.

"Well, 'tis the season, isn't it?" Larry winked. "See you at 9:30. Spread word. Don't be late!" Larry was a stickler for punctuality.

Zach roamed back to his office. His mind was spinning as he started unpacking his bag. He opened his laptop, checked e-mail, and started his weekly TO-DO list. In actuality, he was on autopilot, utterly preoccupied with curiosity over the coming meeting. As he opened his iPad, James' card fell onto his desk. *Must add that to the list.* "Call James G from Gram's church—Haiti."

Pulling his phone from his coat pocket, he had a voicemail. His heart raced.

It was Maggie. "Hey, welcome back! Hope you and Henry made it back with no fender benders this time." She giggled. "Yea, anyway, give me a shout. Would love to meet up in the next couple days."

Zach's head was spinning. *What in the world does she have to say to me? Okay, just call her.* He was coaching himself into another step of courage. He tapped her number on his phone.

"Hey there!" she answered with her characteristic, marvelous Mags spunk. They exchanged quick greetings and Henry updates. Thanksgiving Day was never mentioned.

"How about dinner and shopping?" Mags asked with enthusiasm. "I still have a bunch of stuff to knock off my list, and I'd love to go to the city. How about Thursday evening?"

"Sounds great. How about I pick you up at 6:15?" Under normal circumstances and with any other companions, Zach would have preferred a trip to the dentist over shopping in downtown Philly. But this was Mags, and she was eagerly asking for an evening with him.

"Great. And we'll talk details before Thursday. Gotta fly. It's a full day of appointments for all my vets and our furry friends."

As they hung up, Zach found his own vibes to be more jumbled than ever. *She wants to go to the city with me, and she seems to be her sweet, spunky self again. It feels like normalcy. But what was she up to on Thanksgiving Day and why didn't she tell me? What in the world is her dad up to? He's uncharacteristically jovial, especially for never-jolly Larry Brinkley.*

Brinkley. Meeting! 9:30! Zach jolted back to real-time.

It was 9:29. Zach grabbed his iPad and went sprinting for Larry's office.

CHAPTER 10

Starfield

Travel tales from the long weekend blended with curious queries over this out-of-character, quickly-called meeting. The big table was buzzing with the chatter of colleagues as Zach came bounding into the room. The older veterans of the design-firm were clustered at one end. The rookie, Alex, was seated with the younger crew.

I'm good. The boss isn't even here yet. Zach was relieved to discover he was not late. Just then, Larry Brinkley entered the office.

"Hear ye! Hear ye! Welcome back, boys and girls." Larry was carrying one very large, glistening-gold gift bag, which he placed at the center of the table. A sudden silence came over the team of seven architects. The bag's handles appeared to be tied shut, tightly adorned with a thick strand of red ribbon.

"I know you're mighty curious why I called this meeting." The typically oh-so-serious, no-nonsense businessman was sporting a wide smile and exuding the enthusiasm of a kid on Christmas morn. "THIS is why!" He was pointing to the golden gift bag.

"Let me tell you a little story and read you a letter. Then it will all be clear." He grinned like the cat that had just swallowed the canary.

"On Friday, I came in for a few hours just to plow through a few things. You know, nobody here, so I could get some stuff done."

Of course you did. Smart man. Zach chuckled to himself. Mags had told him that her dad hated Black Friday shopping almost as much as he did.

"Mid-morning, I was deep into reviewing the Alvernia plans. All of a sudden, I heard a pounding sound. I tried to ignore it, but the noise got louder. Eventually, I realized that someone was at the front door." All eyes were on Larry as he rehearsed the tale.

"Standing at the door was one very scruffy, rough-looking fellow—tattered, tan coat, and a patchy beard."

"Sounds like a rather unsavory homeless dude," Alex chimed.

"That's exactly what I thought at first," Larry affirmed, pointing in Alex's direction. "I was about to hightail it back up the steps, when he held out this gift bag and grinned immensely."

"Oh, wow!" Zach blurted out. "That's seriously creepy." Everyone started laughing and exclaiming various opinions about Larry's sanity. "You very well could have been stabbed," vocalized one of the older female team members.

"I know. I know. Hold on," Larry responded. "The look on this guy's face was so genuine. His eyes spoke to me. So I unlocked the door and invited him inside." A couple more of the senior architects were shaking their heads in utter disbelief at Larry's lack of safety awareness.

"Anyway, I know it sounds risky. Get over it. I'm still standing. Our office building was not blown up. Just listen to what happened. Joe, the scruffy fellow, shook my hand and handed me this big gold package and matching envelope."

Larry reached into the center of the table and lifted it by the ribbons, revealing that it was heavy. "Scruffy Joe warmly instructed me: 'Read these instructions carefully. Do not open this package until all of your architects are meeting together next week.' Then Joe smiled big and wished me an early Merry Christmas!"

"Oh, wow. This is good!" Zach exclaimed. "So what's the letter say? C'mon! Are you going to read it?"

Larry exuded a huge smile, "Yes, yes. Here goes." Removing and unfolding a single page, he turned it toward them to reveal a handwritten, seven-line note, with cursive flair. He flipped it back over and read aloud:

'Tis the season—with exceptionally good reason—
Sincerely our best, for sharing and caring.
Choose your brightest three for dreaming and scheming.
Create something truly beautiful, fit for a king.
Bless others, and I will give richer blessings.
Joy spreading wider—
More people will gloriously sing!

"Oh, great!" Alex slouched further in his chair and shoved his hair across his moppish forehead back out of his eyes. He was registering his disgust. "It's one of those devilish riddles to solve, with clues and all. I've heard of these blasted games before. It's SO annoying—a big waste of time."

"Hold on. Patience, young Padawan," Larry urged. "There's more."

He continued reading. Apparently, there was further explanation, written in smaller print:

"Your firm is cordially invited to design a special proposal. This is a two-part, Christmastime challenge. Any three employees from your firm may participate. My five favorite architectural firms have been invited. Please note that your involvement may lead to wonderful, joyous outcomes."

"That's *it*? You gotta be kidding." Alex was unimpressed. "Have you seriously not opened this yet, Boss?"

"Not a peek," Larry responded. "But here goes, right now." He reached for the ribbons.

"Sir, WAIT!" Zach interjected. "You know this could all be one massive hoax, leading us down a big old rabbit hole. Who knows? How can we know this is legit?"

"Well, I wondered the same thing, but if you look close, you'll notice something intriguing." Larry turned over the thick notepaper, revealing the sealed impression. "Whoever hatched this scheme took the time to have it notarized." He sent it around the conference table, so the entire team could examine it.

"It's legit, indeed. This notary is just five blocks from here. We've used them on legal docs several times."

"Okay," Zach responded after examining the notarized document. "Let's go! What are we working with here?" He was anxious, and everyone but Alex was chuckling at Zach's childlike enthusiasm to dive into the mystery.

Larry pulled the ribbons.

The golden bag fell open, revealing a rectangular wooden box, very old, with an antiqued finish. It was reminiscent of a treasure chest. Several ornate pieces of tarnished bronze graced its sides, including a plated keyhole. Larry tugged to open it. It was locked tight. Turning it over, there was a message inscribed on the box's underside. It simply read:

"Design introductory renderings for a top-notch, full-service, walk-in medical clinic, including ER, to be situated on a prime, one-acre +/- lot in northeast Philly. (Site plan TBD). No pricing/bidding. Just plans. Submit at least five conceptual pages of renderings, postmarked by 12/7 to Starfield Project, PO Box 777, Valley Forge, PA. PS: Key to follow if we approve your plans."

The senior architects started shaking their heads. Zach was grinning and running his hands back through his curly hair at a nervous pace. He was thinking. Alex just sat there slouched in his chair, sporting that *what-a-waste-of-my-time* look.

"Is this Starfield business on anybody's radar?" one team member inquired.

"Nothing—I just googled them," another responded. "Only some musical group—no developer or corporate enterprise to speak of."

"What the heck does the freaky poem mean?" Alex blurted his disdainful question. "Seems like we're just letting someone send us on a wild goose chase. Who knows if anything can actually come from this?"

"Well," Larry responded. "I spent the weekend pondering that very question. It seems to me that someone wants to spread extra Christmas joy—big blessings and kingdom anticipation—and they've chosen to let area architects bid via their most creative plans, minus traditional pricing."

"Bid *for what*?" Zach queried.

"Who knows, but this challenger promises to give more blessings and cause many people to sing. Sounds to me like it might be something full of sweet surprise."

There was silence. Everyone was contemplating. Alex was still examining the notary's seal.

"SO!" Larry squared his shoulders. "I've evaluated our current work assignments, and I'm assigning both Zach and Alex to this unique challenge. We don't have the luxury of reassigning your other work, but I think you two gentlemen have the energy and creativity to tackle it."

"Awesome. I'm in!" Zach was thrilled.

"Okay, here we go." Alex was miserably faking some slight interest.

"Who else?" Zach felt deeply honored to be recognized as a dreamer and schemer. He was excited to hear who else was dubbed as such by the boss.

"Well, Zachary, I can't let you young guys have all the fun. I'm putting myself on this one. I'm assigning myself as the third musketeer."

Oh man, what a collaboration of forces. Zach was suddenly musing. *Mags' dad and the pouty, blah-boy Alex, plus ME! If a proposal can come together with the three of us, it will be a Christmas miracle!*

CHAPTER 11

Anticipations

Amid the normal buzz of busy projects, plus the added pressure of the mysterious Starfield Christmas challenge, Zach had managed just a few meager moments for texting Maggie. His schedule was jam-crammed, and the week was flying. It was already Thursday evening, and he was on his way to pick her up for their evening in downtown Philly.

Just show up. Pick her up, and follow directions—easy as that. Zach had learned that if Mags got an idea in mind for an outing and he said yes, she'd have it all planned. He felt some butterflies but he was on his way, driving Henry. And he had to admit that he had been truly anticipating this evening together.

She bounded out the front door with joyous spunk in her step and a festive wreath in her hand. Her hair tossed in the cool breeze. There was a nip in the December air, and though it felt like it could flurry, Zach noted there was nothing precipitous in the forecast. Mags wore her bright red scarf with a blue-plaid, wool blazer. She was beautifully dressed for an evening of shopping. The curly-haired, debonair, young architect couldn't help but think she was a sight for his overworked sore eyes.

"Hey!" She grinned with her greeting.

"Hey there," Zach responded and reached to hug her like he'd done all through the fall. She hugged back, but he couldn't quite read the embrace. *Maybe that was heartfelt, as real as their wondrous walks, hand-in-hand together prior to that Friday before Thanksgiving. Maybe that wasn't quite the same. Or maybe you're just overthinking it all. Lighten up. Be courageous, dude. You got this—Lord, help me be cool this evening.* It was a silent but oh-so-serious prayer.

"What's with the Christmas wreath?" Zach asked. Mags was toting a midsize, deep-green pine wreath graced with a red velvet ribbon. It almost perfectly matched her scarf.

"It's for Henry! It's his get-well gift."

"For Henry?" Zach was smirking. "What's he supposed to do with a wreath?"

"Wear it!" Mags was laughing as she moved quickly toward his tailgate.

"Here you go, buddy!" She threaded the wreath's wire through a slight gap by the tailgate latch. It cinched tight and perfectly covered the dent and scratches created by the bite from Bubba's big truck back in Bellville.

"Oh, are you serious, Mags?" Zach was rolling his eyes and shaking his head.

"Absolutely! It's like a bandage on a dog's tail. The pup might not like it, the dog's owner might not like it, but he's sure to heal faster." Mags had a knack for carrying her veterinary heart into all sorts of other relationships, even with vehicles, and especially with Henry. She had a special love for this old Ford. And these days, Zach was wondering again if she might actually love Henry a little more than she loved him.

They pulled out of Mags' neighborhood, made a couple turns, and zipped onto the Schuylkill, headed for Philly. Though it was rush hour, they were oblivious to the traffic on the just-like-normal, jam-crammed highway. There was so much to catch up together, and it was all pouring out between them. The colorful blow-by-blow of Bellville, Marshall's ax accident, Thanksgiving at Gram's, and certainly Uncle Clyde's urging Zach to revisit Bethlehem.

"So what did he claim you would discover?" Maggie asked.

"That's what's fascinating. I would have been happy to just feel a little more of the Christmas spirit, but Uncle Clyde insisted I could discover faith-filled courage, anticipation for God's kingdom mission, jubilant joy, and more gracious generosity. That's what he said. And so far, a whole bunch of events, conversations, and my personal thoughts have been stirring in those exact ways. It's proving to be quite intriguing, really. Say, where specifically did you want to hang out this evening?"

Zach knew she had something precise in mind. She always did. They were already over halfway down Route 76, headed into the city.

"So, I *was* thinking." Mags had an edge of excitement in her voice. "It's been years since I went to Wanamaker's—well, now it's Macy's, you know. When I was a little girl, we'd take the train into the city at least once during the holidays and shop there. They have the big light show, and they still play it a couple times each evening. Nearby, there are pizza and hoagie shops."

"That sounds fabulous!" Zach responded with great enthusiasm, thrilled to hear how much Mags was excited to be on this adventure with him.

"Oh, and I hope you don't mind, but at some point we might have a little company." She said it with a funny mix of anticipation and trepidation over Zach's response.

"Really?" Zach shot back cautiously. "Who else is coming?"

"Well, possibly the new guy, Alex—from the firm. 'Found out this afternoon that he and his great grandmother, Noni, have plans to be downtown this evening. He asked what I was doing and if we could meet up." Maggie grinned. "That's okay, isn't it?!"

"Sure, no problem." Zach was trying to play it so cool but deep inside, his temperature was rising. "So, um, Alex? Has he been hanging around much with your dad and getting to know you guys?" He was seriously attempting to sound nonchalant.

"We've chatted a few times when I've bounced in the office to see Daddy. Mid-fall, when I did that photo shoot for the new marketing piece, Alex came along. He's a nice enough guy, and he came Dad's way with very high recommendations." She was reading Zach's not-so-well-covered vibes, and she was deeply deliberating if she should spill the beans about Thanksgiving Day.

"Oh, yea, yea, big potential with him. I absolutely agree. Your dad wisely invited him to help us on the Starfield Christmas Challenge." Now Zach was working overtime to mask his brewing jealousy. It seemed like an opportune time to change the subject. "Say, where'd you eat Thanksgiving dinner?"

Zach could not possibly know how his question drove smack dab into such a collision of events. There was silence and, within a few beats, the vibes in Henry's cab felt very awkward.

Maggie gave a sheepish grin and swiped her hair back over her ear. "Well, actually, Alex invited me to his family's for their afternoon and evening festivities. It was really quite the spread."

She proceeded to rave over the family's brownstone, the seasonal décor, scrumptious food, and highbrow guests. She was talking profusely, but Zach had entered a different state, now comprehending little if any of her ramblings. Instead, his thoughts were brewing and bubbling. *I simply cannot believe this! Now it's all making sense. She's infatuated with Alex. Why Alex? I knew I didn't like the guy.* He could feel his blood pressure rising. He was steaming inside. *I anticipated this evening was going to be one thing—just Maggie and me. It's proving to be entirely another.*

He seriously contemplated how every fiber of his being wanted to turn Henry around and deliver Mags straight back to her house. Instead, he gripped the wheel tighter and kept driving straight into the heart of the city.

Advent Week 2: Reflections and Exercises
on Kingdom Anticipation

1. Are there ways you can relate to any of Maggie and Zach's anticipations and frustrations?

2. Read John chapter 1, verses 1–18 along with Genesis chapters 1 through 3. Compare and contrast these passages. Share your own best discoveries, incorporating Doc Ben's insights.

3. How might Jesus' arrival as your King impact your overall attitude and motivation in your relational interactions as well as your daily responsibilities?

4. Explore Luke 2.8–14. Why might the shepherds have needed fresh courage? What do you think the angel meant by "good news that will bring great joy to all people?"

5. What surprises you about the curious, mysterious Starfield Challenge?

6. Join family or friends to watch the movie *The Chronicles of Narnia: The Lion, the Witch, and the Wardrobe*. Discuss together how you see kingdom anticipation presented throughout this classic tale.

7. Identify two or three ways that such *kingdom anticipation* can impact your own feelings about your daily work as well as your approach to special events during this Christmas season.

ADVENT WEEK 3: DISCOVERING JUBILANT JOY

CHAPTER 12

A Fresh Dose

Macy's at Christmastime was magical. Enormous golden wreaths graced each pillar. Even the great eagle statue in the entryway appeared most regal. The base was adorned with lush greens, and the sound of classic brass carols filled the shopping atmosphere. For a few brief moments, Zach's mind actually forgot about the sorry, jumbled state of his relationships, both with Mags and Alex.

Maggie had received a text from Alex, saying that he and Noni would meet them for pizza, but they were still forty-five minutes away. "That's no problem," she texted in reply. "We'll go ahead and squeeze in the very next light show. How about we plan to meet you at 7:45 at the eagle, and go from there?"

This was all feeling rather rushed, invasive, and rude— from Zach's perspective. They settled into the crowd at the base of the light show. As the performance began, Zach was distracted. *Why does she have to be so rude? I've been reduced to chauffeur status. Unbelievable!*

Then, as the music and lights synchronized and grew in volume, Zach's attention felt strangely arrested. Focus was suddenly jolted. The explosion of lights triggered his imagination. He was remembering the scene again—from the passage he'd quoted as a middle school student. "Shepherds were in the fields … the glory of the Lord shone around them … and they were sore afraid … the heavenly host declaring … glory to God in the highest!" It was all flooding his psyche, and he was pondering. *I wonder if this explosion of lights and music might just be a little taste of what those shepherds experienced that night on the hillside outside Bethlehem. That must have been breathtaking, because this is certainly amazing.*

As the show was finishing, he was suddenly jolted back to the store floor, realizing that Mags had placed her arm inside his. She was up close, oh-so-close now. *What in the world!? How's a guy supposed to make any sense of this girl?*

As the crowd dissipated after the show, Mags and Zach made their way toward the big bronze eagle. Alex and his great grandmother were nowhere to be found. They waited. *He's late.* Zach thought to himself. *Sure sign of a slacker.*

At 7:50, Alex texted that they were just landing in the parking garage due to traffic. *Now it will take them ten more minutes to find their way into Macy's.* Zach was ruminating. "I'm starving!" he announced with more than an edge of impatience.

"Zio's is worth the wait!" Mags beamed. "And remember, Noni is Alex's GREAT grandmother. She's spry for her age, but she won't be winning any races as they get here."

When they finally meandered into the lobby at 8:05, Alex and Noni exchanged hugs with Maggie.

C'mon. Enough already. Zach was annoyed.

Once seated at Zio's, they ordered an extra-large specialty pie and drinks. A thick thread of awkwardness dangled in the air. "So tell me your thoughts about this special project, Zachary." Alex's great grandmother was trying to break the ice. "Alex tells me it's very mysterious and rather pesky to your already-full deadlines right now."

"Pesky, eh? Is that what you call it?" He grunted in Alex's direction. "Well, I for one think it's a fun diversion. I'm making some progress on *my* portion of the plans and really find it fascinating and rather marvelous, for multiple reasons."

"Really!?" Alex said with his own tone of back-at-cha. "You would. It's right up your daydream-loving alley, for sure. What could possibly be marvelous about such a time waster?" It was obvious to everyone that Alex must have not been making very much progress on his pages.

"Well, for starters, it's just creative and unique enough to add some real pizzazz. Who knows whose big office the whole grand adventure comes from OR where it might lead us? Hopefully, we'll pick up some great work and impact in the near future! But the seriously wonderful thing to me is what it's done for Mags' dad. He's so enlivened by the potential of a new project for down the road, plus the hopefulness of engaging in this bless-more business. I find that he's actually fun to be around right now. While work is still tough everyday, I've got greater anticipation about it."

Mags started laughing. "True! That's very true. It's funny you say this about Dad, because often, already by this point in the holiday season, he's a real grouch, even downright unbearable to work with."

"It sounds to me like he's taken on a fresh dose of joy," Alex's great grandmother interjected. "You three kids know about joy, don't you?" They stared at her for a moment. Their faces told a tale. They were intentionally working extra-hard to process what she was asking.

"Well, I know the word gets tossed around a good bit," Mags chimed. "Especially in the marketing business this time of year. Stores use campaign slogans like "Spread the Joy" in order to encourage people to buy more gifts. Seems that joy has become synonymous with more spending and more material goods. And I sometimes stage family photo shoots where the kids are holding big letters or blocks that spell out JOY."

"Yes, I realize that's the way joy gets thrown around these days," Noni responded. "But joy, real joy, ends up being the cardinal characteristic of all of yuletide. Back in the original Christmas story, some of the characters were faced with gigantic obstacles and a very big decision. Will I stay stuck in fear, shrink back, sink in dismay, or choose to rejoice?"

The pizza had just arrived. As they started sinking their teeth into their first slices, Noni continued. "It's the Gospel writer, Luke, who spotlights joy in his accounts. God's angel, Gabriel, appeared to the very old priest, Zechariah, as he worked in the Jewish temple. It was a stunning message—he and Elizabeth would have a child. That was such a shock—both Zechariah and Elizabeth were way past childbearing years—this elderly priest struggled to believe it. Later, Gabriel appeared to Mary. She was a very young woman, probably just a teenager and from a relatively poor family. The angel told her that she would conceive by the Holy Spirit and give birth to a son."

"That had to have been *a lot* to take in," Alex commented. "Most of us raise our eyebrows *today* if a gal in her teens tells everybody she's pregnant. We think—what kind of a girl is she? If we don't ask it out loud, we think it." Everyone snickered.

"Yes, so imagine finding out you're going to be expecting," Alex's great grandmother continued, "and there's not going to be a human father. AND your child will be God's son. And on top of all this, you are to name him Jesus, which means Deliverer."

Maggie jumped in. "I think that would be a pretty heavy responsibility to carry, an awfully big burden."

"Yes, this had to have felt extremely heavy," Noni affirmed. "And it's extra heavy when you remember that God's people—Mary and Joseph's people—were dominated by Roman rule, under the political system of the Roman emperor. The Jewish people had spent many decades watching, waiting, and anticipating the arrival of their Messiah, a great King who would deliver them."

"Wait a minute. So this was actually rather revolutionary, right?" Zach was seeking clarity. "I've never thought of this in such a subversive light. This had to have felt like they were signing up to lead a political revolt."

Noni was grinning. "Yes, yes indeed. It could have most certainly produced a strange mix of emotions, including all-out fear, despondency, second-guessing, and great apprehension."

"In reality, it is a VERY big deal that Mary replied, 'May it be to me, according to your word.'" Maggie was correlating with rapid-fire connections. "She really had every reason in the world to say 'No way' instead of 'Yes.'"

Alex just sat there listening, quite noncommittal regarding his take on things. His great grandmother was leading the thought train. She lowered her voice now, as if she were telling a secret. She had the other three's rapt attention. "Real joy is much more than a feeling, though extra-good feelings can certainly be a byproduct. God's style of joy is a deep-in-your-soul, jubilant gladness because of God's gracious, life-changing work. Because God is working in us and through us, we can make the choice to rejoice."

"So whatever our circumstances," Zach added enthusiastically, "it's a healthier, more intentional choice of attitude, whether times are wonderfully happy or horrifically sad. We can choose joy!"

"Exactly right," Noni agreed. "And wrapped all around these scenes, the various characters encountered joy. Elizabeth, wife to Zechariah and relative to Mary, was expecting. Her baby *leaped for joy* when Mary entered the scene and spoke. Mary herself broke into a song, often called her *Magnificat*. In this magnificent poetic utterance, she declared, 'My spirit *rejoices* in God my Savior.' Her song's backdrop paints a picture of oppression, poverty, and despair for God's people. But instead of caving in, she made the choice to rejoice. When Elizabeth's baby was born—we read this at the very end of Luke 1—Zechariah exuded joyous praise. The same exuberance characterized the shepherds' response to the heavenly hosts when they learned of Christ's birth. They bubbled over in joyful praise."

"Sounds like quite a different emotional slant on the season." Alex spoke up. "In contrast to just more purchases, more money, or more gifts under the tree, this understanding of joy sounds like something with a good bit more meat on the bones."

"Yes!" his great grandmother affirmed with delight, "You're grasping it, Alex. Right on target! And such joy has the potential then to spread to others, to coworkers, to clients, to family, and neighbors. We might say joy has the potential to be contagious."

They had utterly devoured the pizza. As the dust was settling from the lively conversation, they took inventory. Each of the ladies had eaten only a single slice. Alex ate two, and Zach admitted he had polished off the rest. "No surprise there!" Mags exclaimed. She gave an affectionate punch in Zach's direction and leaned her shoulder closer to his.

They said their goodbyes as they headed out the lobby doors at Zio's. A messy mix of slushy drizzle was coming down. Zach looked to the sky and grimaced.

"You kids be careful driving home," Noni instructed.

"We will, don't worry about us," Mags reassured her. "We've got trusty old Henry to get us safely home."

CHAPTER 13

Joy at Work

Back on the road, Zach was driving extra-cautious. After the incident last week, he couldn't help but feel a bit apprehensive maneuvering through such a mix of sleet and freezing rain. He turned the knob on Henry's old retro radio and started scanning. This required an old-fashioned, tiny turn of the knob instead of auto-scan.

"Better see if we can catch a weather update," Zach explained. All he could find was Christmas music, so he landed the dial on one of Philly's easy listening, pop stations.

"I find Noni's proper manner and careful words to be so mysteriously captivating. What did you think of her?" Mags asked.

"She's fine—very fine. It's the great grandson I can't stand." Now it was out there, and not an ounce of question dangled in Mags' mind regarding what Zach might think of him.

Mags feigned a smile. "Now, Zachary, have a little charity. He's really not all that bad a fellow. I think you need to give him some time. Perhaps he'll grow on you."

"Perhaps you're right." Zach realized that he'd said too much. "But then even mold can grow on you." He chuckled at his own wit but started quickly recalculating. "Anyway, his great grandmother's description about joy was certainly intriguing. I've never thought about joy as a deep choice of gladness, rooted in God's gracious work in and through us. And it just makes sense that such an attitude change is exactly what your dad is experiencing."

"Yes, I think you're right, Zach." They both noticed that the wintry mix had begun to lessen in intensity. The traffic was moving at a bit steadier pace. Henry was handling the road famously.

"What's amazing is also what Noni said about joy being contagious. It's been true in my own life. Because your dad's overall tone has been more joyful, my week has been more positive and productive. And this thought hits me, Mags." Zach was speaking with excitement in his voice. "Joy is mentioned by Apostle Paul as one of the Holy Spirit's fruits—one of those outcomes, a byproduct of living a Christ-honoring, loving, kingdom-oriented life."

"That's a sweet connection, awesome strands of truth weaving together," Mags concurred. "And something else. Think about this! Oh wow—" She said it with that just-connected-the-dots, eureka tone in her voice. "*Joy to the World*. It's possibly the foremost, seriously famous Christmas carol of all time."

"Yep, great point, Mags." Zach was nodding and still gripping the wheel very tight.

"But contemplate several of the key lines." Mags softly sang: *Let earth, receive her King.... No more let sin and sorrow roam, nor thorns, infest the ground.... He comes to make his blessing known.... far as the curse is found, far as the curse is found.*" As she was singing it, Zach realized that she had inched her way across Henry's bench seat. They were almost shoulder-to-shoulder again.

"Wow!" Zach exclaimed. "Several ideas are zinging my way. Here's the kingdom anticipation all over again, much like Doc Ben and I were talking about in the church café. The King has arrived, so his kingdom has been inaugurated. Of course, it's not fully here yet. There's so much more to come! But it *has* begun."

"I think I'm following, but you're saying it like there's more," Mags coaxed him.

"Yes, here's more of that impetus, a big-time motivation to reverse the curse. Doc Ben insists that it's not simply a matter of Christ himself having come to create such a curse-reversing effect. Yes, the Father's planning and sending of his son is certainly exceptional work. But as his kingdom citizens, it's also now *our* role to work to accomplish royal new things that reverse the curse. We can be—we should be—bringing greater joy to the world as we actively lead in endeavors and serve others."

"Oh, boy, I'm getting it!" Mags exclaimed. "I'm wondering how I've missed this all along."

"Ah, don't feel bad, Mags. We've all missed it. We readily enjoy the Christmas tunes, which are great, but we seldom slow down enough to actually process the biblical messages that can be seen in the lyrics."

"So if we play this out, more people can experience this genuine, deep joy when *you* design really good buildings, and *I* care for pets and their owners with exceptional service. Right?" Mags was checking her trail of thinking. Zach was nodding and smiling.

"And the curse is reversed—more joy spreads across the world—as researchers discover new treatments for disease, as entrepreneurial farmers develop bright, eco-sensitive methods of producing even more food for the hungry world, and as teachers cultivate young minds." Zach was on a roll.

"Of course, don't forget, great car guys reverse the curse and bring a lot of joy when they turn wrenches, repair, and restore vehicles. Can you imagine our world today without the likes of a Henry?" Mags patted the dash, as if she were petting her favorite canine. Zach shook his head and rolled his eyes.

"It is rather amazing," Zach reflected, "to realize that every Christmas season puts up a great big sign—a virtual billboard, really—reminding us of how the King has arrived, and we can be busy doing kingly, joy-filled, world-changing work as citizens in the kingdom."

Ironically, in that very moment, Josh Groban's version of *Joy to the World* began playing on Henry's classic, silver-knob radio. "Okay, what are the chances of that? Is that cool or what?" Mags chimed in enthusiastically. "Gives me goose bumps!"

"Odds are actually pretty strong that someone's rendition of that song would be played during our hour-long trek out of the city, when you consider that after all, it IS Christmastime, Mags." It was Zach's extra-realistic sarcasm, at his finest.

"Okay, you don't have to be such a killjoy, Zachary David. You, ever the rational, uber-analytical, would *of course* insist on ruining my moment." She smirked and pushed away from him just enough to slug him in the arm. But then she moved even closer and put her head on his shoulder for the final stretch of the journey back to Valley Forge. In that moment, Zach concluded without a doubt that this evening was ending with immense joy.

CHAPTER 14

Help

Act like Joseph. You did it before. Do it again.

As they rolled down Maggie's road, Zach had this deep-in-his-soul sense. It was time to apply faith-filled courage again in this relationship. They pulled into her driveway. He put Henry into PARK. Instead of hopping out to walk her to the door, he swallowed hard, took a deep breath, and said, "This turned into a seriously marvelous evening, Mags. May I ask you something?"

"Absolutely! Anything," she said with a warm smile. She shifted on the seat bench just a bit in order to face Zach. He resisted his urge to turn Henry's engine off. It was chilly enough—they might get cold—and though he was eager for a more substantial conversation, he did not want to come across *too* eager.

"So help me figure this out, please." Zach was leaning forward, arms and hands on the steering wheel. He was shaking his head. "I realize I am typically a little crazy, but you're really driving me even crazier than ever." Zach nervously ran his fingers back through his curly locks.

Mags was grinning. "What do you mean? What's wrong, dear?" She put her hand on his, just over top the steering wheel. "I'll help you figure it out."

"I'm trying to figure *you* out, Mags. Do you want to be with me? Or do you now want to be with Alex?" Suddenly, a part of Zach couldn't believe he had blurted that out.

"Just a few weeks back, I felt so confident about you, about me, about *us*, really." He almost dared to tell her he'd actually looked at engagement rings, but he pulled back. It was quick silence, split-second apprehension along with his second thought. *It's one thing to be courageous. It's another thing to foolishly tell all.*

Mags opened her mouth to respond, but Zach was staring out the front windshield, and he plunged ahead with his torrent of thoughts.

"I rolled into the Christmas season feeling so jumbled about things. The firm's finances have been tight and stressed, so mine have felt so much tighter as well. Then I've had this haunting feeling, like I've not really changed much in terms of my workplace influence. We came off those amazing weeks last summer—after Grandpa's funeral and our talks with

Doc Ben, Gram, and Marshall—with such focus and passion to reach others with Christ's love. I was so fired up to be on mission with Jesus in the everyday opportunities of work, but then—"

"Hey, listen, you're not alone on that, Zach." Mags said it with genuine empathy. "I've felt the same frustration. When we were first back, late summer and early fall, I was doing so well with demonstrating loving care to my pet owners. 'Even had some great conversations about faith, the kind that felt like they might go somewhere in the future, but then—"

They both chuckled, realizing their similar feelings of personal frustration over unmet aspirations in their workplace influence.

"I can't say I have a fix-everything answer for you," Mags interjected. "We both know we want to serve Christ and others in ways that truly make an eternal difference. It's especially a poignant feeling this time of year as we recall Christ's passionate purpose and big mission in coming to earth. I think we need to focus our efforts together more, pray more fervently, encourage each other more, and gain some fresh insight and motivation together in these areas for the coming New Year."

Zach's personal psyche quickly locked onto her "together" language. In those moments, he felt his hopefulness was returning, and now even stronger.

"And I'm so sorry I can't fix your financial stresses either. Heaven knows I'd love to snap my fingers and see Brinkley Design-Build fully flourishing again. 'Would be so good for both you and Daddy. I catch his feeling-low comments, including the up-too-early mornings and his burning the midnight oil in order to multitask, cut costs, and otherwise make that bottom line work, somehow." Zach was appreciating her empathy and by now, their hands were linked together on the steering wheel.

"I can't help with any of that thick jumble of fears, Zachary." She paused, and Zach thought he caught the glistening of tears in her eyes. "But I *can* help you with your other questions."

Zach gulped inside and braced himself. "You can?" Their eyes locked and hers seemed to peer deep into his soul.

"Yes, I can. I can indeed." She said it with the utmost seriousness. "Right before Thanksgiving and then in joining Alex's family for Thanksgiving, I was sorting some things out. I guess you might say it was serious soul-searching. I'll admit I was a little bit intrigued by Alex. I felt like I needed to chase things a bit."

"Chase *him*, you mean?" Zach snorted.

Mags grinned, "Okay, yes, maybe just a little." She tipped her head and swiped her hair back over her ear. "A little jealous, are we?"

Zach hung his head and chuckled.

"It was only a very few days," Mags reassured. "And then after listening to Alex and watching his family, do you know what happened?"

"What?" Zach replied. His emotions were quivering deep inside. He hoped she couldn't feel it in his hands.

"I couldn't help but think about *you*." There was a catch in her typically confident voice. "Midway through Thanksgiving Day, I found myself wondering how things were going at Gram's and how much fun you were having with all your cousins. I was thinking about what Marshall and Doc Ben were up to, and even how your Uncle Clyde might be pontificating and afflicting everyone with some goofy old, guilt-inducing phrases."

Zach started grinning with a very broad smile. "Are you serious? For real?"

"Yes!" Mags shot back. "And all of this helped *me* realize, I just can't imagine—I'm very serious—I can *not* imagine my life without you, your amazing heart for Christ's adventure of serving and blessing others." She squeezed his hands tighter and pulled closer to him on the truck bench.

A wave of fresh confidence washed over Zach's heart and mind. Based on these amazing responses from Mags, his thoughts were racing about their potential future. This generated even more questions, but he realized these would have to wait for another conversation.

"And of course, one other big thing you need to know."

"What's that?" Zach asked.

"I can't imagine life without Henry either." Mags grinned.

"Of course you can't."

Henry's headlights were still on, and it seemed as if they were shining even brighter now.

CHAPTER 15

Grace Golfs and Risks

There it sat, right in the middle of the conference table. As Alex and Zach entered Larry's office early Friday morning, they saw the locked-so-tight wooden chest. It was the next step in the Starfield Christmas Challenge. If their proposal won the favor of the mysterious challenger—whoever he or she might be—they would win the coveted key. They could then open the antique box and hopefully move on to participate in some sort of Christmas blessing.

"Let's do a quick status update," Larry explained. "How are your portions—your sets of pages? Based on the preliminary concepts and footprint we sketched together on Monday afternoon, how are your plans coming together? Who wants to go first?"

Zach revealed his exterior plans. Classic red brick blended with keystone-style block work, accented by uniquely placed contemporary windows. His plans were truly stunning, and Larry gave him the 'atta-boy, thumbs-up.

Alex hung his head and sported his sulking, mildly apathetic look. He revealed what he had created so far. Though he felt uncertain about his progress, Alex had actually accomplished more than either Larry or Zach might have imagined. Of course, his interior plans included several glass curtain walls. Larry made certain to give him kudos as well as some coaching on additional steps to take. Zach gave an internal shrug and said nothing. *What a chump. Who knows if he'll really pull this off?* Zach was failing to resist his own compulsion toward snarky musing.

"All right, we're going to put a bow on this by Monday morning and make certain it's postmarked and certified so as to hit the Tuesday deadline, right on the money. That means I want your full attention, both of you, totally wrapping up your pieces this afternoon. I'm doing the same with mine."

"Sounds great, Boss," Zach affirmed. "Thanks for inviting me to be in on this. It's certainly all very intriguing, and who knows what's going to come of it, but it does indeed spice up the whole work season right now with some good doses of joy!"

"That's right, and to add some further joy, if we successfully wrap this up by midmorning on Monday, I'll treat you guys to lunch and a round of golf."

"That sounds like serious fun!" Zach exclaimed.

"It's supposed to be unseasonably warm on Monday, upper fifties, maybe even low sixties and sunny," Larry explained with anticipation.

"I suppose I could suffer through a round of December golf," Alex glibly commented.

Friday proved to be fuller than expected. All three of them pushed through the weekend, working feverishly on their sets of renderings. Midmorning Monday, Alex was nowhere to be found. Finally, Larry received a text from Alex. It simply read: "Plans are printed, lying on my desk. All good."

Larry located Alex's printed renderings. All was not so good. Upon reviewing them, there were glaring errors scattered throughout. He and Zach successfully retrieved the renderings from the files and made the necessary corrections. Zach groaned and grimaced with each stroke of the keys. Hitting print, they joined them with the other sheets, rechecked everything one more time, and bundled the set. Rolled and tubed, Larry carefully sharpied the label just as previously instructed: Starfield Project, PO Box 777, Valley Forge, PA.

Alex was still nowhere to be found, so Larry sent him a text: "Let's meet at Shannondell. 12:15 sharp. Lunch at Chadwick's. Then golf."

"We can take my G37," Zach suggested. "Feels like a sunroof day, for sure." They headed for the post office, sharing a sense of triumph with their accomplishment of the proposed plans for the Starfield Challenge.

As they drove, they exchanged questions. *Do you really think they'll like our plans? Will we get a key to open the antique chest? How soon do you think we'll know? What's the potential of this whole thing being one big hoax?* Zach could not resist asking this one, of course, distinctly revealing his own penchant for pessimism. And the biggest one of all—Larry said it, "I'm totally at a loss for who this grand schemer might be. Which of our business clients could have set up such a challenge?"

Once they arrived at the clubhouse, they put their name in at Chadwick's for lunch—a ten-minute wait. "Not bad, not bad at all," Larry commented. "Gives just enough time for Alex to get here, even if there's a little traffic." They were counting on walking up to golf without a tee time. After all, it was the middle of the day on a Monday.

They were seated. 12:15 came and went. No Alex. 12:25. Still no Alex.

Larry texted. Nothing. Zach texted. Still nothing. They went ahead and ordered off the lunch menu. It was very evident to Zach that Larry was not pleased. *I've known this all along,* Zach mused. *He's a chump, a slacker—a real bump on a log.*

As they started munching their burgers and fries, they resumed their questioning. "So do you think our mystery challenger is indeed already one of our clients?" Zach queried.

"I think it's a possibility, but I'm sincerely not sure. I've been racking my brain trying to figure out whom I know that is business savvy, a creative thinker, *and* crazy generous. I get the impression, based on the poetic riddle-clue, that this next step involves something that generously blesses people. Lord knows, more of that needs to happen. AND Lord knows that this mix of business acumen, creativity, and generosity, well, it's a rare combo in leaders."

"Good point, Boss. So what do you think? Will Alex meet us for golf?"

"Who knows!?" Larry shook his head. "Perhaps, but I don't think we need to text him any further." They headed for the golf course. As they were paying, both of their phones chirped. It was a text from Alex: "Can't make it. Unexpected surprise development. Have fun!"

"That's it?!" Zach was reacting, only this time he wasn't keeping it inside. "What exactly is an unexpected surprise anyway? I thought that by its very nature every surprise is unexpected. He's both an idiot and a chump!" *Did I really just say that out loud?* Zach was immediately regretting his words as they rolled off his lips.

"Okay, let's go!" Larry was eager and just a bit annoyed. "The days are getting shorter and we're wasting sunshine."

They got out on the course. It was indeed a much nicer-than-normal December day. Sun was shining. Temps were holding steady in the low sixties. They each had a solid shot off the opening tee. It certainly did not feel like Christmas time, but there was nothing serious to complain about. They were golfing.

Rolling along toward the second hole, Zach could not hold it inside any longer. "So, why in the world did you hire Alex, and why do you keep him?"

Larry rolled his eyes and chuckled. "That's a great question, Zach, seriously a great question, especially in light of today's escapades. There's actually a rather unique and simple answer to that. Strange as it may sound, God has been working on me over the past couple years about being more gracious and letting his grace have a serious place in our workspace."

Now he had Zach's full attention, especially in light of his own stirrings and frustrations in recent months. "Okay, I can trek with that," Zach responded.

"One of the things I've been sensing—and I think this is from the Lord—is my need to involve younger leaders on our team." Larry was confidently explaining and seeking to read Zach's vibes, all at the same time. "I've been moved to take some carefully discerned risks and deliberately hire a few guys and gals who might still need to encounter Jesus, his gracious and life-changing work. Then, with these new employees in our mix, I want to share the Gospel and potentially help them trust Christ for new direction and purpose."

Zach was silent for a few beats, just staring and obviously contemplating.

"If I'm honest, God's been nudging me in similar ways, ever since last summer when we walked through everything with Grandpa out in Ohio. I came back, excited to be very mission-focused in my approach with clients, coworkers, and other contacts. 'Was good for a few weeks. Then my enthusiasm started to wane, and then Alex came onboard. He and I failed to hit it off, and it's been downhill ever since."

"Your lack of a bromance hasn't gone unnoticed around the office," Larry commented with a wry smile. "Let me tee up and hit away."

CHAPTER 16

It's a Wonderful Missa

Larry rocketed the ball—a beautiful shot. It was Zach's turn. He teed up, swung hard, and watched it fly— all the way to— just past the ladies' tees. Zach dropped his head and resisted his all-out urging to toss his clubs into the nearby stream.

"I didn't mean to shake you up with my comment there, Zachary."

"Ah, it's okay." Zach was shaking his head, stunned that he let himself become so bothered. "I just want to get a better handle on this whole business of blessing others and really being loving toward others so I can more effectively reach them with Christ. And it stings a little when I realize how I'm blowing it with Alex."

"Well, cut yourself a little slack," Larry said it with a tone of empathy. "It can already be extra hard for the best of us to apply grace to a fellow with Alex's overall disposition. But then, for you, when it appears he's trying to move in on your girl—" Just like that, Larry halted his words. Now he was the one stating too much. He couldn't believe he let that slip, especially when it involved his own daughter.

Zach said nothing and just grinned. It was still an awkward moment. Up to this point, he and Larry had never spoken directly about Zach's relationship with Mags. Things were kept "strictly business" between boss and employee. In this moment, they both quickly landed back on that side of the invisible line.

"Especially here at Christmastime, I'm reminded of how important it is to generously extend God's grace. It's at the very core of what Christmas is all about. Last year, something I was reading—'don't remember exactly what—reminded me that the root idea behind Christmas, 'Christ's mass,' originally carried the very heartbeat of mission. 'Mass' originally meant more than a church service with holy communion. The word came from the Latin word *missa*, meaning 'sent out.' It was more about the *dismissal* from a church gathering, God's people *going out on mission*, compared to the worship service itself."

"I've never, ever considered this!" Zach exclaimed. "It's fascinating."

"I agree," Larry continued. "So I was struck with this insight. Consider it with me. Christ was sent down from heaven to us, bringing God's joy-producing grace. And so, Christmas can and even *should* motivate us. God is sending us out to bless and reach others with his grace and joy. Our *being sent* to give God's joy and grace, well, it's right at the heart of Christmas."

Zach had managed to clean up his game as they moved into holes three and four. The conversation was proving to be deeper and richer than any of their talks together in the past. And Zach really felt like Christmas came early when he birdied the ninth hole.

"There's something else that's stirred my thinking in recent years," Larry continued. "It's the old movie, *It's a Wonderful Life*. 'Remember it?"

"I think so. I've probably watched it a few times plus a collection of clips when I'm channel surfing each Christmas season," Zach answered as he was fixing his divot.

"What I viewed for many years as simply a feel-good Christmas flick has morphed in my thinking in recent days. George Bailey's desperate personal struggle now conveys great wisdom for discovering personal significance in my daily work.

In spite of the movie's title, George's life seemed anything *but* wonderful. As the story opens, we learn that George is thinking about taking his own life. Plagued by one setback after another, the guy had struggled for years with feeling unhappy, discontent, and purposeless."

"Based on my conversations," Zach interjected, "so many people struggle day in and day out with those same feelings."

"Exactly! George and the entire Bailey Building and Loan enterprise endlessly wrestled with doing what was right—selflessly serving others—and yet not being able to get ahead. George Bailey *does* consistently make right choices, but again and again he's filled with regret and seethes inside with raucous feelings of pointlessness and emptiness—even jealousy and anger—over others who seem to succeed and have easier lives. For George, intentionally working to do the right thing feels difficult, lonely, and fails to land him in first place."

Zach was nodding and reflected further, "Even as we focus at Christmastime on Jesus' coming and his joyful, serving heart, we can easily feel conflicted. We are busy and pushed with extra demands and distractions. We feel the crunch of end-of-year expenses and deadlines—I know I certainly do. We encounter the relational strain of coworkers and family who are frazzled and grumpy. We even wrestle with déjà vu, easily recalling the "ghosts" of Christmases past, those years that were less than snow-globe-like."

"Yes," Larry agreed. "A few such ghosts have haunted me over the years. George Bailey knew these feelings all throughout his life. But if we pause to reflect deeper, we discover that George Bailey's story shows us how God uses ordinary, struggling, disturbed, fearful, down-on-their-luck people to change the world."

"What do you mean by that?" Zach questioned. "I'm curious where you see that. God has been working on me, motivating me to be more courageous, more kingdom-focused, more joyful, and more generous. I'm beginning to see with greater clarity how each of these can indeed be world-changing, in a sense. But how do you see that in this movie?"

"Here's just one example." Larry was excited to share. "Clarence the angel showed George what life would have looked like if he'd never been born. Bedford Falls was now Pottersville, a dismal place. No one recognized him. No one. He and Mary's grand old house was nothing but an old shell, in shambles. He ran through the house, shouting for Mary and the kids. No one answers."

"Oh yea, that scene always gives me the shivers," Zach exclaimed with recollection. "When he goes to his mother's house, she answers the door. She looks so old, rough, and haggard, and she does not know him. No one in town recognizes him."

"That's right," Larry continued. "George stumbles upon a graveyard and finds his brother, Harry's gravestone. Clarence shows up and tells him that Harry drowned as a little boy in the pond. George shouts a flamboyant denial, 'I pulled Harry from the icy water that day. Harry's alive! He's a hero. He rescued all the men on that transport!' 'No,' Clarence retorts. 'You were never born, George. Every man on that transport died. You see, *you* weren't there to save Harry.'" Larry paused.

The silence on the golf course felt oh-so-reflective for both of them.

Neither of them could believe it. They were already on the sixteenth hole. "I think it shows us how God still uses everyday, ordinary people in the process of sharing his amazing mission of redemption and transformation. Though we may never completely know our full impact during this lifetime, George Bailey's example highlights how important our roles actually are in our daily workplaces."

"I love it," Zach chimed, "when George ends up back on the bridge, praying and pleading, 'Please, oh God, let me live again. Please, I want to live again.' And at that moment, he is restored—and it starts snowing again—'love that part! With great jubilation he heads home and discovers that Mary has rallied the townspeople, who all bring money to bail out George and the Bailey Building and Loan. The house is jam-packed with friends, and in the closing scene, George's hero-brother, Harry, arrives and makes a toast, 'To my big brother, George, the richest man in town!'"

"Yes, and notice *why* he's the richest man in town. George has been *so* gracious, extremely generous, working from the personal posture of vibrant others-orientation. George has been leading his own life and the Bailey Building and Loan with the aim of sincerely blessing other people."

"I want to do a better job—be much more intentional—about cultivating joy, grace, and generosity in my outlook and actions." Zach was voicing personal ownership for his own next action steps. "I'm going to start by asking Alex if he wants to golf with me sometime soon. I'll see where the conversation goes and how God might already be working in his heart."

"That's a fabulous idea." Larry was smiling. "Good luck getting him to show up on time!" They both chuckled.

"Now don't misunderstand me," Larry clarified. "I cannot endlessly tolerate employees doing sloppy work and engaging in tardiness. There are indeed standards of excellence to uphold. But I'm attempting to take a more nurturing, joy-expressing, grace-extending approach with at least a few employees each year, all with the aim of glorifying God, reflecting his joy, and hopefully reaching a handful of young leaders like Alex with Christ's Good News."

As they were wrapping up the eighteenth hole, Zach declared: "This afternoon has been glorious. Great conversation, great golf, and great weather. It's just fine by me if it stays like this in early December, but give it a week or two and I'll be ready for some white stuff!" To Zach's dismay, there was not a trace of snow in the two-week forecast.

CHAPTER 17

Grand Opening

With a brisk chill in the air, the silver courier vehicle parked in front of Brinkley Design-Build at 2:15 on Wednesday afternoon. The midsize, padded, manila envelope was simply delivered to the front desk, and the receptionist's signature was sufficient. She had been instructed to immediately bring any unique deliveries or messages, "Anything out of the ordinary, directly to my office. Please interrupt any meeting in order to get my attention." Those were Larry's exact instructions.

He held the slender package, giving it a light squeeze in an attempt to discern the contents. Nervously and excitedly he tore it open, and within moments, he was calling for Zach and Alex to join him. As they rushed in, they could read the good news all over his face.

"Here it is, boys! We got a key!" Both guys beamed great big smiles.

It was a slender, old school, skeleton key. Larry passed it around.

"So you didn't open the box?" Alex wondered aloud.

"No, no, I *had* to wait for you gentlemen. All three of us have skin in this game."

"Was there any kind of note, or just the key?" Zach asked.

"Simply this—a printed out half-sheet." Larry read it aloud: "CONGRATS! Here is the key. Enjoy your next steps."

"That's it?!" Zach exclaimed.

"That's all," Larry replied. "No signature. No letterhead. No real clues. Hopefully what we find inside will give us something more to go on." He took the key from Alex, picked up the antique chest, and started for the keyhole.

"Hold on!" Zach halted him. "Before we open it, anybody else want to place bets on what we're going to find?"

"Maybe it's a check, a nice fat deposit toward our work on the clinic plans." Alex was imagining. "That's what I'm guessing."

"That'd be nice!" Larry was laughing. "Heaven knows we could use that for some cash flow cushion right now. But I seriously doubt this works that way."

"Right," Zach agreed. "That would be too simple. The note mentions 'next steps,' which leads me to think there's something more to do in the challenge." Zach was ever the strategist.

"That's probably the case," Larry agreed, "but maybe there is *some* money in there, a sort of reward. Remember the little

riddle that came with the big gold bag ... um, what was that?"
Larry shuffled through some papers there on the conference
table and came up with the note. He read it again, aloud to the
other two:

Tis the season—with exceptionally good reason—
Sincerely our best, for sharing and caring.
Choose your brightest three for dreaming and scheming.
Create something truly beautiful, fit for a king.
Bless others, and I will give richer blessings.
Joy spreading wider—
More people will gloriously sing!

"For sharing and caring ... Bless others, and I will give—"
Larry was pondering. "This makes me think there's some
serious charity involved. Perhaps there is a check with a nice
amount to give away to a needy family or a certain group in
our community. Wouldn't that be cool to do? Kind of like a
pay-it-forward bonus, spreading a different kind of joy on the
heels of winning the contract."

"But do we actually know that getting this key signals
that we've won the contract?" Alex was asking the cold, hard,
reality question. Larry raised his eyebrows. Zach said nothing,
although he couldn't help but make his own private note. *Alex*
might not be as dim-witted as I've come to assume.

"Well, there's really only one way to know." Zach was
smiling big. "Better open it up and see, Boss."

Larry placed the key in the hole and gave it a turn. There was a click, and then what appeared to be a puff of dust emanated from the hole and edges of the lid. The open lid revealed two curious objects inside. One was wrapped in wax paper.

"What the—what in the world do we have here?" Larry puzzled. He pulled back the wax paper, finding a small rectangular block, like a bar of soap. But it was a gummier substance with a fragrant smell, and it glittered.

"Okay, that's, ah, interesting." Alex was unimpressed.

"What's that one?" The second object was tucked in a weathered, dusty, canvas pouch. "Go ahead, take it out, Zach." Larry coached him.

Zach loosened the cinched leather cord and extracted a small old juglet, rough-hewn in texture, and deep tan in color. "This has the appearance of something from a far away land, perhaps Roman, maybe Babylonian, who knows?!" Zach was seriously puzzling now. And then they noticed there was a cork in the neck.

"You've got to be kidding," Alex interjected with a tone of amusement and intrigue. "That's just begging to be opened."

"What are we gonna find, our genie in a bottle?" Zach was chuckling.

"How many wishes do we get?" Alex volleyed. They were actually talking to each other, understanding each other's quirky humor, and maybe even enjoying the interchange.

Zach pulled the cork. To their shock, it opened easily. He peered in and passed it to the other two. There was a thick liquid inside, with a musky scent about it. Alex thought it stunk. "Ugh—that's odoriferous. Cap It quick!"

Zach liked the smell. Thus, they had quickly found something new on which to disagree. As he was recorking the juglet, it slipped from his hand, spilling some of the substance on the conference table.

"Come on, man!" Alex jeered. "What a klutz!"

"So, we've got a block of some glittery, gummy stuff, and a spooky old jug with Aunt Matilda's regifted liquid soap from Bath & Body Works." Zach's sarcasm was kicking in. "Whoa, wait a minute, what's that?" Zach exclaimed. "There on the lid."

He flashed on his phone's light. Across the inner side of the dusty lid, Zack could barely make out a faint image:

"What in the world *is* it?" Larry asked.

"Great question," Alex replied. "I didn't know we were getting sent on a treasure hunt. This looks like one of those 'X marks the spot' maps, taking us to something buried."

"Well, in a sense, we hoped it was truly a treasure hunt," Larry quipped. "At least I was hoping we'd find some golden business somewhere along the way."

"Um, I think there's something more here." Zach was shaking his head, still shining his light on the underside of the wooden lid. He began wiping thick dust away from the image.

Suddenly, lines of additional, faintly painted text emerged. Zach started reading aloud, as he was able to slowly make them out:

Fit for a king, more hearts will sing.
Choose a place in need of his grace.
Bigger plans to bless the mess
Make them reach beyond the US
Design your dreams—move past charity.
Mark them with dignity and sustainability.
Build them to last, far-reaching indeed.

"You've got to be kidding!" Alex voiced his own frustration. "I thought we were done with riddles and clues, we'd be granted the design contract, and now we would take off with full development and drawing of official plans for the medical clinic."

"Yes, this is all getting a bit more complicated than I envisioned." Larry was echoing Alex's sentiments. "I'm starting to think someone is just playing around with us. 'Seems we are wasting a lot of time that could be poured into projects we actually know will yield some positive financial results. This appears to be a pipe dream!" Larry slammed the lid shut, as if to say, "DONE!"

"Hold on!" Zach pleaded. "Just a minute. I know you guys are frustrated. But let me take this on, Boss. I promise to not drop the ball on the rest of my projects."

Alex had slouched back in his chair and was rolling his eyes.

Squinting his own eyes, Larry slid his glasses up on his nose and stared intently at Zach. He was deeply contemplating. Just then, there was a tap on the office door. "This just arrived." The receptionist handed Larry a simple white envelope. "Some guy, pretty scruffy looking, with a patchy beard, wearing an old coat. He said you might be needing this about now, and that I should tell you that Joe says, 'Hello and Merry Christmas.' He made me nervous at first, but then he turned out to be friendly enough."

Larry moved quickly to the window. Glancing at street level, he recognized the man walking down the sidewalk as the same man who delivered the original gold package and explanation back on Black Friday.

He opened the envelope and read aloud: "Your initial concepts for the clinic are masterfully designed. We want you to demonstrate if you can think beyond borders, for blessing people in even greater need than those nearby. If you have not already done so, explore the wooden box's cover carefully for further specs."

"Hey, at least we're headed the right direction," Zach interjected.

Larry continued reading: "Please respond with your best plans—no designs or drawings this time. Only words. No more than five pages. Send again to the Starfield address, postmarked by December 21. Enjoy dreaming!"

"Okay, I'm personally frustrated and apprehensive about this whole challenge."

"That makes two of us, Boss!" Alex readily saw the splendid opportunity to agree with the big man *and* potentially get out of additional work, all at the same time.

"If you really want to keep chasing this, Zachary, it's yours. I'm curious for the challenge but no longer so intrigued I want to keep going myself. Go for it. Just make sure you're still getting your other projects finished. We need cash flow."

"Will do! You got it!" Zach said it as if he knew exactly what to do. While he was responding with great moxie, he was actually taking a big gulp deep down inside. At best he had a handful of hunches, but no actual confidence regarding what direction to head next. Zach's synapses were firing fast, and he needed to catch his breath. He had learned across later summer and early fall that one of the best ways to clear his mental clutter and focus better was to take a long drive behind Henry's wheel. He was determined to do exactly that when he got off work.

Zach was doing his best to stay on his tasks, even with so much busy brain. He was wrapping up his afternoon projects—it was 4:45—and he estimated another twenty to thirty minutes should do it. His phone chirped. It was Mags.

"What are you doing when you get off work? Want to hang out?"

Advent Week 3: Reflections and Exercises
on Jubilant Joy

1. What's been your own concept of "joy" in the past, especially during the holidays? Why?

2. How might Noni's explanation—and this way of describing joy—potentially change your own perspective?

3. Explore Luke's Gospel, chapter 1. Where does "joy" emerge and how does it impact the original Christmas characters?

4. With your family or a group of your friends, watch the classic Christmas movie *It's a Wonderful Life*. What do you discover about genuine joy?

5. Is there an "Alex" in your life right now (possibly two or three such people)? Can you identify someone who pushes all your buttons, but you sense God nudging you to extend greater grace and exude more genuine joy toward that person?

6. What steps might God be urging you to take in order to share his joy, grace, and love with others this Christmas? Make some specific plans.

7. Could your workplace stand some extra doses of joy this season? What could you do to be more genuinely jolly, like Larry?

8. Plan for something surprising, extra-fun, and joy-filled you will spontaneously do with family or friends in the next few days. Spread the joy!

ADVENT WEEK 4: DISCOVERING GRACIOUS GENEROSITY

CHAPTER 18

Kingmakers

Enormously therapeutic. Zach had learned that taking Henry on a long drive could be so restorative, but even more so if Mags was along. He was delighted she wanted to join him. It would give him the opportunity to catch her up on the day's big developments and to gain her insights. Such a drive would also grant him more time to discern next steps in their relationship.

Ever since their clarifying conversation last Thursday evening, Zach found himself hopeful again. He was even thinking more seriously about possibly proposing to her. He knew he had taken some very definitive steps of courage in the past couple weeks, but *engagement, now that would be seriously Joseph-like, big-time—very gutsy indeed.* He could not help but muse as he headed to pick her up.

He also could not help but wrestle internally over the lack of ample money in his bank account. *I probably have saved just about enough money to buy a ring and a few other Christmas gifts. But things are so tight—any cushion I've built up will be gone. I really do hope that next year is a more productive year.*

With such thoughts, he typically autocorrected, rechecking his own emotions and doubling back to remind himself. There was no need to rush into things. *After all, just last week I had the distinct impression that she cared more about Henry and Alex than me. Watch out for where your excitement takes you, man!*

As he picked up Mags, she strolled to the back to inspect Henry's wreath. "Still looking good," she said, grinning. "You're healing nice, old fella!" She patted his tailgate. They zoomed down the road.

"Where are we headed?" she asked.

"Oh, you're actually going to let me decide for once, eh?"

"Yea, there's a first for everything. It must be the Christmas season is softening me up a bit. Don't get used to it."

"Don't worry, I won't," Zach quipped back. "Might sound like a stretch, but it's still early evening. Let's go to Lancaster. We can be there in just a little over an hour."

"I'm game," Maggie replied. "Sounds like fun."

As they drove, Zach caught her up on the details—the skeleton key, the box's two strange objects, the mysterious image on the lid, the poetic clue, and the further note explaining a couple more details.

"It sort of makes sense, I think, Mags. If I'm breaking it down correctly, the aim is to design a way to bless people in a spot that needs real help—outside the United States. And it seems this challenger-developer wants to seriously back such an endeavor if it's a well-thought-out strategy."

"That makes sense, perfect sense based on what you've described and read to me. And it's so cool to see such big generosity being expressed by a business leader. It seems extremely sensitive, kingdom-minded, and Christ-honoring."

"Yes, that's all true, but I've got no clue what direction to actually roll with this." Zach was running one set of fingers through his thick, curly hair while gripping Henry's wheel with the other set. They were zooming out the PA turnpike and making very good time as they drove.

"I'm remembering one of our conversations last summer with Doc Ben," Mags reflected. "He mentioned how certain leaders are working to develop plans that actually advance business, create jobs, and strengthen economic growth in needy global regions. And hand-in-hand with such strategies, further spiritual momentum is being cultivated among participants in the businesses, on multiple levels and relationships. I wonder if that's not a big part of what the challenger means by 'more hearts will sing.'"

"Hmmm. I think perhaps you're right on track with those connections, Mags. It seems this creative developer wants to truly live out the Christmas spirit in the fuller sense of *missa*, the people's mass, and our being sent out on mission with

Jesus." Zach started chuckling. "I still can't believe how Uncle Clyde's push for me to journey back to Bethlehem has been playing out this season. I've seen Joseph and his courage more clearly, as well as the Gospel writers' emphasis on kingdom anticipation. I revisited Mary, her relatives Elizabeth and Zechariah, as well as the angels and shepherds. They all ended up choosing jubilant joy, even in the face of some oh-so-somber circumstances."

They were merging into traffic on Route 30, rolling across the northern edge of Lancaster. "How about we hit up Prince Street?" Mags suggested. "Great sandwiches and tremendous coffee."

"Ha! I knew that your letting me make our plans could not possibly last the whole trip." Zach shot back.

"Ooops!" Mags was grinning, "You chose Lancaster. I just figured you were now open to ideas on where we should actually eat." She grinned and punched his arm.

They drove down Route 222 and landed at Prince Street Café. Ordering sandwiches and drinks, they sat at a high-top table in front of the long row of front windows. Crisp December air accentuated the scenes of the season. The road was bustling with holiday traffic. Sidewalks carried a brisk hustle of shoppers, as well as people arriving for the show across the road. *White Christmas*, the classic musical, was the season's featured production at the Fulton Theatre, which stood directly across from the café.

"I wonder when it will snow," Zach was wishing, "at least a little bit of the white stuff in the next couple of weeks. 'Makes it feel more like Christmas."

As their sandwiches arrived, Mags broke from their chatter about the sights and sounds of Lancaster. "So a thought hits me about your Christmas blessings challenge."

"What's that?" Zach asked.

"You know how you can easily recall the angels and shepherds scene—you can still quote it word for word?" Zach was nodding and taking a bite out of his scrumptious panini. "Well, I have some big memories from one of my Sunday school teachers—I was probably in middle school at the time. She taught us some unique details—so unique I've never forgotten them."

"Okay, and this has exactly *what* to do with the price of tea in China?"

Mags grinned. "Patience, patience, my dear. I'll explain." Sinking her teeth into her Reuben and sipping her mocha, she noticed there was an ever-so-slight hint of precipitation in the air outside. *Was that a flurry or freezing rain?* she wondered silently, but chose to not mention it and get Zach's hopes up.

She continued. "The mystery package—the gift bag and treasure chest with the glittering bar, dusty jar, and the clues on the lid—I'm wondering if that's all supposed to remind us, even point us, toward something more." Zach was giving her his own classic clueless, I'm-not-following-your-logic look.

"I have a hunch. Now hear me out carefully. My Sunday school teacher all those years back gave us these fascinating facts about the wise men in the original Christmas story. Like, did you know there's a good chance they had traveled for over two years from a far-off place like Babylon?"

"I knew it was far away," Zach replied, "but I've not heard the idea that they were from Babylon." He bit into another crunchy mouthful of turkey and cheese.

"Yes, there are clues in Matthew's Gospel that reveal they were likely official leaders—they were called *magi*—sort of spiritual guidance officials in the Babylonian government. A big part of their role was discerning, recognizing, and dubbing new rulers. In a sense, you might call them kingmakers. They were likely from a long line of *magi*, or wise men as we commonly call them, quite possibly dating back to the time of Daniel, way back when the Israelites were in exile."

"Wow, I've never heard of that link," Zach responded. "They were seriously a long way from home. 'Must have really been sent out from God and into the *missa* thing." Zach laughed at his own quirky, intellectual joke.

Mags chuckled as well. "Yes, yes, Zachary. Now you are actually following the thought train. Welcome aboard!" She slapped him a high five, and their hands stayed close as they landed back on the table.

"My teacher—I think her name was Mrs. Greider— explained that these wise men likely discovered the ancient prophesies buried among Daniel's writings. Having some insight from those sacred truths of the Messiah to come, and then receiving the prompting from God through the star in the sky, they would have headed out to find the promised king."

The waitress returned, and they each ordered some tea to go. Zach and Mags agreed—the evening's adventure wouldn't be complete without walking the downtown sidewalks and soaking up the seasonal sights of Lancaster.

CHAPTER 19

Fit for a King

Stepping through the expansive glass door facing onto Prince Street, Mags noticed again the ever-so-slight hint of something in the mid-December air.

"Could it really be snow, Zach? How cool would that be this evening?!"

"Don't get your hopes too high, Christmas Girl." There was a sudden, big gust. Zach caught her wind-blown scarf and then wrapped his arm around her. "My weather app shows the temp's rising back into the mid-to-upper 30s in the next hour. This little flurry stuff is likely to be rain or even icy mix in a few minutes. 'Could be an interesting drive home for Henry."

They began walking up King Street, in the direction of the Convention Center. Mags was about to resume her Sunday school lesson.

"Okay, I'm following you," Zach jumped in before she could. "But what does this nice little trip from Babylon have to do with our mysterious box?"

"I think it has *everything* to do with it!" Mags replied with great gusto. "You see, the *magi*, these kingmakers, brought gifts, and scholarly tradition says that their three gifts each had meaningful significance as they were given to Christ."

They had stepped inside the doorway to browse one of the shops near Central Market. While quickly looking in storefronts and otherwise window-shopping, they were remaining fully engaged in their conversation.

"What do you mean?" Zach asked.

"If I'm remembering what Mrs. Greider said, the gold was the gift that represented his royalty, the frankincense honored his deity, and the myrrh acknowledged his humanity." They were both silent.

"Oh, my word!" Zach exclaimed. "The gold-colored bag ... and the wax paper wrapped around frankincense, and the juglet is holding myrrh ... so, these are gifts—"

Mags chimed in to say it with him, "Fit for a king!" They said it together with a sudden sense of epiphany.

"Wow! Yes," Zach exclaimed. "The package and box contents match up with the lines in the poetic clues. Our challenger is very witty indeed."

They had turned several times in their walk, with no real strategy to their direction. At this moment, Mags realized they were on Queen Street, just a few feet away from Ream Jewelers.

"Hey, Zach, come here." She said it with a giddy, excited-little-girl tone in her voice. Zach followed blindly, only to suddenly realize they were now window-shopping in front of the jewelry store. They were staring directly into a display full of glittering diamond engagement bands. Quickly, Zach was feeling nervous. *Oh, my, this could be awkward.*

"Check it out!" Mags exclaimed. "Is that amazing or what?!" She was pointing at a midsize, elegant gem nestled atop a classic setting.

Zach stared into the case and took a no-big-deal sip of his hot tea. Steam rose from the cup lid, blending with the wintry mix of light flurries. "A lot of gold bling in that window," he commented in a nonchalant manner. In spite of his casual posture, the ring's style was duly noted as he took a mental photograph.

"It's gorgeous!" Mags volleyed.

"And you are even more so—" Zach was suddenly stunned, mildly embarrassed, and wondered to himself how in the world he came up with such a romantic statement.

Mags blushed, grabbed his coat, and pulled close to him. They locked hands, turned, and headed back toward Prince Street.

Lamppost light was reflecting golden hues against all the storefront windows. Suddenly, Zach's app proved dismally reliable as the flurries took on a much damper feel. Within moments, the two of them were dodging through a messy mix of sleet and rain.

"So much for the snow. Henry is parked just up around that corner," Zach declared as they picked up their pace. Once inside Henry's cab, he started the engine and moved the lever for some heat. Maggie moved closer to Zach on the seat bench.

As they rolled up and out of Lancaster, their conversation returned to the ancient kingmakers in Bethlehem. "So gifts like that, fit for a king—the thought strikes me, Mags—these wise guys demonstrated Uncle Clyde's key themes. They were courageous to make the journey. Obviously, they held kingdom anticipation, and their generosity with such gifts was amazingly profuse."

"And don't forget," Mags interjected, "the story reports that when they saw the star, they were overjoyed. Mrs. Greider taught us about a stack of joy words there in Matthew's Gospel. It adds up to mean, 'They rejoiced exceedingly with great joy.' And all of this was in the face of real controversy, serious conflict with paranoid Herod and the apathetic religious leaders. Such stressful circumstances remind us that the *magi* made a choice to rejoice."

Henry was rumbling along the turnpike, but at a reduced speed due to the slushy mix. "This connects a bunch of the dots," Zach was reflecting. "And it helps me grasp more of our challenger's intentions, heart, and creativity."

"Definitely," Maggie agreed. "But what about the writing on the underside of the box lid? And what do you think you're going to propose?"

"Yea, I'm pretty stumped on what it means and what to do."

"I have another thought," Mags said with a gleam in her eye.

"What's that? This ought to be good." Zach was grinning.

"This seems like the kind of job for Doc Ben. Why don't you call him—get his input? I bet he'd be game to help."

"Hmm. That is genius, Maggie. Pure genius. I think I will first thing tomorrow morning."

CHAPTER 20

At the Center

Bright and early, six o'clock on Saturday morning Zach picked up Mags, and they were on their way. Doc Ben had agreed that this was a conversation worthy of a face-to-face meet up. No phone call could possibly do it justice. Zach had tried texting him a picture of the box lid's inscriptions, but the pictures all came across too blurry. Doc felt he needed to see the mysterious symbol and painted letters in person.

Zach had what he hoped might prove to be another stroke of genius. Back in the office on Thursday morning, he had encountered James' business card. The card went tumbling out of a stack of notes by his computer. Zach had barely given James and his development ideas for Haiti a second thought, but the card's sudden appearance grabbed his attention.

In light of the blessing challenge, the mysterious message on the box, and now this stumbled-upon business card, Zach couldn't help but wonder how God might be working. After hanging up with Doc Ben and agreeing to meet halfway on Saturday morning, he prayed a deep prayer, asking for Christ's direction, and he placed a call to James. To Zach's shock, James answered, and stunningly, he had Saturday free and was able to join Doc Ben for the ride over into Pennsylvania.

Mags and Zach buzzed along in his G37. Although Mags had begged for them to take Henry, Zach insisted he needed some rest. "The hour-plus drive to Lancaster was probably enough exercise for his old bones for one week, Mags. Gotta give him a breather. Anyway, I'm in more of a sports car mood for Saturday. And we'll make better time on the turnpike."

They enjoyed smooth roads and, of course, great conversation, reviewing all of the various details. Mags wanted to break down the clues once again and rehearse the *magi* connections. They picked up piping hot, large teas at one of the rest stops, which fueled their thinking and dialog in even greater ways. And of course, they mused over the pirate-like symbol's meaning. Zach even bounced some of his ideas off Mags regarding a possible "blessing proposal." His heart and mind were whirling with the kingdom potential of something in Haiti.

Somerset, PA, was the best midway point for a meeting, approximately splitting the eight hours in half for both vehicles. It also provided best options for restaurants. During the drive, they had texted with Doc and James several times. Zach and Mags arrived at Kitty's Corner Café. Sure enough, Doc Ben and James arrived within ten quick minutes.

Hugs and handshakes were quickly exchanged. Zach looked awkward and felt rather self-conscious. He was toting a cardboard box into Kitty's. The box contained the antique chest, to be analyzed by Doc Ben. He knew it wasn't everyday that customers hauled along their spooky antique boxes. *Hopefully, my cardboard box makes me at least slightly more inconspicuous.*

"Thanks SO much for trekking the miles, both of you, especially on such short notice." Zach was big on exuding gratitude. "Frankly, I was shocked that you guys were both game for doing this."

"No problem, Zachary," Doc reassured. "You know my love for such adventures involving the merger of theology and everyday mission."

"Same for me," James affirmed. "Very glad to be included in such a quest, especially if we can figure out how to get you—and you too, Maggie, if you're available— to join our team this coming February in Haiti. We are getting together a great crew from church to go."

Zach could tell that James was in sales. He was not bashful, not in the least, about trying to sell him on the idea of going along. Fortunately, Zach was far enough along in his own thinking that James' strong encouragement was in no way a put-off. He was sporting a big smile. A waitress stopped by their table. They ordered coffees, teas, and fresh-made muffins.

"That's certainly part of what I want to talk to you about, James. I think such a trip may play an integral piece in all of this. But before we talk those angles, we need to see what Doc Ben can make of this." Zach lifted the wooden chest from the cardboard box. Mags cleared space on the table. Both Doc Ben and James chuckled as other customers gave their table amused stares.

"That's unique, for certain," Doc stated as he ran his fingers over the tarnished bronze pieces and the old keyhole. Zach took the key from his pocket. Other customers had resumed their meals, but all eyes at Zach's table were glued on the treasure box. Turning the key and lifting the lid, he turned the whole container toward Doc Ben.

"So what do you make of it?" Zach queried. "Does this symbol make any sense to you—anything you might have seen before?" He promptly began pushing his fingers back through his hair.

"Patience, Zachary David," Mags scolded. "Let the good doctor do his work."

Doc propped his glasses on the end of his nose and brushed his fingers, ever so slightly, over the faded, painted symbol.

"Hmm." It was said in a deliberative, pondering tone. "Yes, yes indeed. It's an ancient symbol—very ancient. I'd need to verify my dates, but I know it goes back centuries now." Doc Ben paused and lowered his voice. "The symbol's meaning definitely holds epic significance for all that you are discovering."

"Really, for sure? Oh, come on, tell us what it means, please!" Mags was enthralled with all that they were encountering.

Doc Ben grinned like the cat that had swallowed the canary. "This particular symbol was used prolifically throughout Christian architecture for many years. In fact, this same emblem was used as ornamental ironwork on every set of stairways at my alma mater. That meant I walked past this symbol multiple times each day across my years at the university. In recent years, it has faded in usage, but the meaning is still powerful."

Maggie was shaking her head. "OKAY, Doc. Enough already. You're killing us here. What's it mean?"

"Wow, Mags," Zach clipped back, "who's struggling with patience now?"

Doc laughed and then got down to business. "These are two Greek letters, deliberately overlaid. The X is the Greek letter 'chi.' It's pronounced *key*. The *P* is the Greek letter 'rho,' and sounds like *row*. Here's how they merge into a simple cipher. These are the first two letters in Christ's Greek name, *Xpistos*.

The other three were munching their muffins, sipping their hot drinks, and hanging on Doc's every word. "Across the centuries, these two letters have been used by Christians to reflect their adoration of Jesus as their *Christ*, the promised Messiah and their empowering King. In fact, come to think of it, still today that's my university's theme: 'Christ is at the center of everything we do.' The *XP* has served as a perpetual reminder that he is at the very center of our mission and the source of all our strength."

"I'm getting it!" Zach was nodding. "Apparently, our mysterious challenger—whoever he or she might be—wanted to emphasize this in a big way."

James couldn't remain silent. "Yes, and don't miss what's on either side of the *XP*. It's the alpha and the omega, the first and last letters of the Greek alphabet. Christ himself said, 'I am the Alpha and the Omega, the beginning and the end.' This was his way of saying, 'I started this grand story. I will wrap it all up, and I am all you need in the in-between. From beginning to end, I am your all in all.'"

"That's phenomenal to remember," Mags reflected, "especially during this time of year as we celebrate Jesus' coming." She said it with soft introspection. "It really should impact how I adore him and engage in his mission all year long."

"That's good stuff, truly tremendous, Miss Maggie." Doc Ben found her correlation skills to be perpetually impressive.

"Hey, so how about we order some more of *this* good stuff!" Zach was pointing at the menu and grinning. "It's lunchtime, and we need some fresh fuel for our talk about blessing more people in Haiti."

CHAPTER 21

Thick Threads

Kitty's Café boasted several Italian specialties. Zach ordered fettuccine with a tomato cream sauce that marvelously blended Alfredo and marinara. Mags indulged in penne with succulent chicken, topped with a simple red sauce. Doc and James ordered double cheeseburgers and cheese fries. All four started with cups of chicken noodle soup. Piping hot with homemade noodles, it was a perfect precursor to their lunch entrees.

Zach devoured his soup. "Scrumptious!" As the others were scooping and raving over the noodles and juicy chunks of chicken, Zach picked up the treasure chest again.

"So, James. It's your turn. I have some ideas, but please tell me how you cipher this and what we might do with it in Haiti." Zach read the lines aloud:

Fit for a king, more hearts will sing.
Choose a place in need of his grace.
Bigger plans to bless the mess
Make them reach beyond the US
Design your dreams—move past charity.
Mark them with dignity and sustainability.
Build them to last, far-reaching indeed.

James furrowed his brow for a moment. "I don't claim to be some great interpreter of poetic clues—nothing close to Doc's skills in ancient languages, history, and all—but I don't think your challenger was trying to be very elusive here."

"What do you mean?" Zach was curious.

"I mean it would appear you've already deduced the first four lines. You're focusing on the King, whose aim is that more people's hearts will enter into his kingdom and experience resulting joy. You're already thinking about a global spot that needs serious blessing and an intentional reverse of sin's curse—that's where Haiti can come in."

"So you think we're on track?" Zach sensed James' words to be encouraging.

"Yes, yes indeed. But I'd say the final three lines are very important to crack." They all gave James a puzzled look. He continued, "I'm not saying it's only crucial to *know* what your challenger means by these words—yes, that's important if you want to win the reward. But I'm talking about knowing how to actually *apply* the meaning, so that indeed more people end up joyously singing in the kingdom."

"You're saying we better know how to move beyond missional theory, to take effective action, so more people truly encounter our King." Zach was following.

"Right on!" James affirmed. "And it's not rocket science, but it is a different way of approaching people. I'm seeing three thick threads right here. You want to make certain your proposal contains these three crucial threads."

Zach pulled out his phone, as if he were going to take notes. "You're welcome to jot things down, but your dusty box lid already holds it all." James grinned. "First, *move past charity.*"

"Okay, see, I find this very confusing." Mags authentically reflected. "I thought that as Christians, we're supposed to be all about charity, and especially at Christmastime."

Zach was nodding and wrinkling his nose in agreement. "Yea, aren't we supposed to be generous and share with others? That line in our blessing challenge sounds like something old Ebenezer Scrooge would say. *Move past charity.*"

"It's a very common and valid conclusion. We are indeed commanded by God to lovingly assist others, helping them out of poverty. Blessing others by giving material resources when people are in desperate need, well, that's very good. Certainly, there's a time and place to mobilize quickly when emergency relief is needed. Natural disasters and other sudden crises necessitate such."

Mags and Zach were listening intently. So was Doc, but with something of that wise-old-sage look emanating across his face.

"I don't think our challenger means we should SKIP or ignore charity. The operative word is *beyond*. Don't let your generosity be *only* a handout. Too often, those of us in the wealthy regions of the world have poured lots of cash, goods, and services into the developing world. We do so with good intentions, and we end up feeling some sense of accomplishment. We feel powerful and good about ourselves. Oh, we may even sense some self-validation out of helping others in the name of Jesus. But that's it, and in many places around the world, the same patterns of poverty just continue repeating themselves for years to come."

"I can see that. I'm following you." Zach took a big bite of his pasta and commented between forkfuls. "What you're describing makes a lot of sense, but how can it be any better, James? After all, we can't *make* people in struggling places be productive, can we?" It was an honest, and impassioned question.

"That's where the second and third threads become oh-so strong in the tapestry. *Dignity and sustainability.* Dignity means we treat people with utmost respect, based on their being made in God's image. Instead of just giving out money or imposing our preconceived notions and programs, a *dignity* approach means we begin by asking people how they are gifted and what they already possess. What resources do they *already* have in hand, skills and passions with which they can bless others?"

Mags jumped in. "This is so good! Instead of approaching people as if *we* are wealthy and mighty—like they really need *us*, and *we* know what's best for them—instead, we help people discover how they can take active steps to grow and thrive."

"Exactly!" James encouraged. "So in the places we work in Haiti, we come into a community asking questions. How are they already skilled, and what are they seriously passionate to accomplish? Dignity recognizes that because of our Creator God, every human has intrinsic worth. Every person, even those in especially messy and struggling places, has special skills, resources, gifts, and abilities. In most developing nations, our approach in starting businesses and being generous should be to *first* tap into people's personal, God-given resources. This actually serves to affirm their dignity."

Doc Ben joined in. "Moving beyond charity and marking the work with dignity really sets people up for sustainability. Right, James?"

"That's right. So even when the business developers pull out several years later—and they almost always do the work continues. People are set up to succeed. Their local economy will continue to grow. New jobs will still be created. And people can continue being reached for Christ."

"Okay, so what's this really look like?" Now, the ever-so-practical, rubber-meets-the-road Zach was talking. "Give me an example."

James started chuckling. "Lucky for you our work in Haiti already holds these approaches. So there's a woman in one village—she joined a savings group. This is one of our leading approaches, helping people learn to save money together. Out of her time in the savings group and her subsequent growth in Christ, she realized God could use her passion for cooking. With a small loan from the group, she opened a roadside stand, a restaurant of sorts. It serves people near a busy intersection, selling food several times each day. As a result, her kids can afford to attend the local school, and her family's house is now being finished."

"That's quite amazing," Mags commented. "So people learn, grow, and develop *themselves*. It's not wealthy outsiders moving in, giving them all the answers, dumping resources and leaving them in the same condition when they're tired of the adventure."

"You got it!" James applauded with a smile. "And with this approach, people's creative ideas and skills can be endless. There are men with roadside garages who repair tires and replace spark plugs. There are clean water stations, building material suppliers, and roadside grocery stores. There are jewelry bead businesses."

"Any diamond dealers?" Mags tossed in her quick question, glancing and giggling in Zach's direction. Both Doc

Ben and James chuckled, picking up on her intended humor at Zach's expense. He simply returned an awkward grin, rolled his eyes, and took another big bite of pasta.

James rescued him with some continued explanation, "Woven through all of the savings groups and business planning is the centrality of the Gospel—Christ's amazingly redemptive work to restore people to their Creator, to creation, and to one another."

"How could our Christmas blessing challenge be involved?" Zach asked.

"Marvelous question!" James affirmed. "A bunch of us from our church actively partner with a leading mission group called HOPE. Their coordination provides oversight and empowering structure for this work in Haiti and many other wonderful places. HOPE is exploring what it would look like to have a resource hub, a center of sorts with winsome leaders and more tools available. While the aim is going beyond charity, toward dignity and sustainability, it still requires generous Christians who will help give of their finances. Those finances could build a culture-appropriate training facility, hire several key leaders, as well as supply further training materials for the growing number of savings groups."

Zach was nodding. Doc Ben was grinning with the realization that the pieces of the puzzle were clicking together. And Mags was suddenly worrying over her extra-aggressive, diamond ring comment.

CHAPTER 22

Journey toward Generosity

Rain, very cold—almost freezing rain—was pelting the pavement. Their conversation was wrapping up as they stood in the café foyer. It was already mid-afternoon. Each group knew they had a four-hour, return trek yet to go. They sensed a newfound urgency to get back on the road, because there was always the potential for a messy mix across this region of Pennsylvania.

"So you've given me plenty of material to write my proposal," Zach declared with a summative and grateful smile. "And Doc, your insights on the box's cipher-symbol emphasizing Christ as King—that's phenomenal. Huge thanks!" Doc Ben nodded with a no-problem posture about him.

"And I think you better sign us up for the February trip. For the short-term I can propose some great concepts on paper for our Christmas challenger's consideration, but I think we need to see things firsthand." Mags loved hearing Zach say "we." Though she had no problem being assertive, she still would have felt like it was over-the-top pushy to just say, "Count me in!"

"I agree," James responded. "I'll send you a link with more details, the signup form, and cost info, just as soon as I get home this evening."

Hugs, handshakes, and warm goodbyes were exchanged. Each vehicle hit the road, heading east and west respectively.

When they were about halfway home, Maggie texted Dad. Larry suggested that she and Zach plan to join him for a mid-evening dinner when they arrived back. "I'll have something in the oven, hot and ready," he messaged. Larry was eager to hear the scoop and catch up on what they had learned.

Zach and Mags' car ride back across the turnpike was abuzz with review of all the day's deep and rich discussion. And of course, there were dozens of more questions. The biggest ones buzzing in Zach's brain could not actually be vocalized to Maggie.

What did she really mean by her grinning diamond-business-in-Haiti question?

Should I take this as my big hint that she'll say YES if I propose?

Am I really ready for this?

And the biggest one of all: *Can I afford to buy a ring right now?* Zach was adamantly opposed to going in debt to buy things, especially something like jewelry.

A unique blend of Zach's highly cautious personality along with his long-standing values of savings and frugality dictated such an outlook and approach to his own finances. *But how does all this match up with being courageous?* As they drove, he was wondering, pondering in the deep recesses of his psyche, even as Mags rehearsed aloud the glorious discoveries they had made through today's conversations.

As they came through the front door, Larry greeted them. "I've got cheesy pasta bake in the oven." Larry started pulling it out, his back to them as they dropped their stuff on the chairs. "'Figured you two could stand something hot and hearty after the long drive and chilly conditions." Mags gave Zach the don't-tell-him hand-swipe-under-the-chin look. Zach grinned and rolled his eyes upon seeing the steaming dish of ziti. They didn't have the heart to fess up that they had already eaten *gourmet* pasta for lunch.

As they ate, Mags and Zach delivered the full scoop, every inch of the details.

"It's fascinating," Larry responded, "a very unique approach to generosity, and yet very meaningful. As I'm hearing it, this makes fantastic sense. It truly does. To first approach people with such a premise, that they are full of dignity because of the image of God in them, and to work off the question— what assets do they already bring? Well, this seems like a brilliant and empowering approach. And it just makes sense that there can be longer-range results for such businesses and discipleship strategies. That has to be what is meant by *build them to last; far-reaching indeed.*"

"Yes, absolutely true, Larry." Zach was nodding. "Hearing these principles and seeing such planning for gracious generosity pushes me to ask what my own next steps of generosity should look like."

Mags was observing how much her dad seemed to actually enjoy and even respect Zach. She could not help but consider what this might be like for the future for them as family—far-reaching indeed. She found herself anticipating, full of joy at the thought.

"So this is sounding like great direction, Zach. And another idea hits me. If these plans move forward, many people can get involved in sharing generously at multiple levels—big, seemingly small, and everything in between." Larry was giving his official, thumbs-up to proceed with writing the proposal. "And I have to tell you two about a couple fresh realizations—what I'm discovering as we talk."

"We've had our share of sudden ahas, that's for sure, Dad."

"Yea, what's your latest?" Zach leaned in with anticipation.

"Well, based on what you've told me—the treasure chest, the golden bag, the objects inside, and their connections back to the story of the wise men," Larry had a gleam of discovery in his eyes. "I'm seeing more clearly how our mystery challenger has very deliberately cloaked his or her real identity, making it even more difficult for us to uncover the source."

"Why's that?" Mags asked with deepening curiosity.

Larry smiled broadly.

"Because of the all-out irony of the mailing address. Think about it. We send everything to 'Starfield Project.'"

Zach groaned. "Oh, *that's good*. The wise men following the star—I get it. Quirky irony, for sure, but it's good."

Mags was laughing. "It's oh-so-creative details like this that make me eager to meet this mystery person."

"So what are your plans for Christmas next week, Zachary?" Larry seemed extra-interested.

"I've been back and forth this week with Gram. She's planning on having a houseful of family come to her place. I'll likely roll that way when I get off work the day before Christmas Eve."

"That's smart," Larry replied. "It will be a skeleton crew for a half day on the twenty-fourth. There's no reason you need to be in the office."

"It will make for a late night of travel headed toward Gram's, but I'd rather avoid the turnpike traffic that day before Christmas. And on top of that, I want to be at Gram's for Christmas Eve. We have several unique family traditions."

Mags was watching him intently. She could not help but admire the confidence and reflection with which he spoke. It seemed the past three weeks had been days of real progress, both for Zach personally and especially for their relationship. What a difference three weeks can make. Mags laughed in her heart when she recalled spending Thanksgiving with Alex.

"What will you and the broader family be doing?" Zach's question was asked in Larry's direction. But of course, his answer would potentially carry intriguing implications related to Maggie. Zach could not help but remember that she had spent Thanksgiving Day with Alex, a memory that did *not* produce the same laughter in Zach's heart, not like it did in Maggie's.

"Plans are still developing, but I think a number of us are heading to see some of my sisters in Jersey." Larry's explanation was nondescript and yet did not seem to welcome further questions.

Maggie said nothing. Naturally Zach was left wondering, and deep down inside, he was oh-so-seriously wishing that she would be with him across those days.

CHAPTER 23

Choices, Cushions, and Courage

Very early on Monday morning, Zachary was the first to light up the office suite at Brinkley Design-Build. He was motivated, focused, and passionate to complete the proposal. *The proposal needs postmarked to Starfield TODAY.* It was at the top of his task list. Sunday had been a full day, but his mind had been percolating on how he would map out the concepts. Now, he felt refreshed and ready to put his thoughts on paper.

Mug in hand, steam was rising from his morning tea. Zach sat at his computer and began typing away. His thoughts were flowing beautifully, and he felt he was fully in the zone. The heart of his proposal reflected the key concepts he discussed with James at Kitty's Café in Somerset. The area to be blessed was a region of villages, approximately three and a half hours southwest of Port Au Prince, Haiti. Committed dollars and strategic leadership would aim to establish a central hub for training Haitian leaders and coordinating the overall efforts of savings groups and new business startups. Zach's plan held multiple bottom lines, including objectives with appropriate metrics for growth, and a very strategic focus on integration with local churches and their faith-based leaders.

These thoughts are flowing strong. Thank you, Lord. Zach had been sincerely praying and deepening his all-out reliance. *I want to sense your hand and sincerely work with you, your leading, and great provision. Help me sense where you're already working and join you right there, Father.* Such requests for guidance were becoming a more regular rhythm in his daily prayers for his work endeavors and relationships.

Zach was already on page three of the proposal. He recalled the instructed limit—a five-page maximum to the proposal. Now that his composition was underway, he realized just how difficult it would be to actually keep this under the prescribed limit.

There was a ding on his screen indicating arrival of a new e-mail. Failing to resist, he gave into his curiosity. It was from James, and Mags was cc'd.

Dear Zach and Maggie,

It was a great joy to meet with you on Saturday. Thank you for inviting me to join the conversation and take part in your Christmas Blessing Challenge. It is one of the most fascinating examples of planning for generosity I have ever seen—and definitely creative!

I know we talked about it briefly, but please accept this as your formal invitation to join the team for our Haiti trip next February. And please find all pertinent details as well as registration information at the attached link.

Cost is approximately $2000 per person. I was remiss to inform you—my sincerest apologies—that the deadline for the 50 percent deposit is the end of this week, December 24. This is necessary in order to expedite all the required details well in advance— especially important with a group this size.

If you have questions, please contact me.

Warm regards and blessings!
James

Uh-oh. Zach's quick mental budgeting clicked into high gear. *With my personal funds as tight as they've been, I don't know how I can pull this off. Oh, boy, what now?*

Under normal circumstances, Zach preferred a personal cushion—anywhere from one thousand to two thousand dollars—a sort of emergency fund in his savings. He realized it wasn't really much of a financial cushion, at least by many people's standards of living, but for a young professional in his twenties, it felt like a healthy amount.

Zach could certainly take the risk—he'd been sensing this would be a Joseph-like move. He could put down the deposit for Haiti. Such a move would be courageous—faith-filled, even generous, indeed—*and* it would make that cushion virtually disappear. This would require new levels of all-out trust in the Lord.

His internal turmoil was torturous. He was wrestling deep in his heart, because he had been seriously toying with taking a different kind of courageous risk—to place a deposit on an engagement ring.

Mags' signals have been so clear, way too strong for me to ignore. In recent weeks, Zach had been aiming to increase his sensitivity to what she said and how she said it. *I know she'd love for me to propose, and especially here at Christmastime.*

He had not foreseen such a deposit being required for the Haiti trip, at least not this soon. *This feels SO frustrating.* Zach was suddenly very distracted from finishing his proposal. *It's such a collision of financial choices. I know it's an opportunity to live out all I've been learning—the courage, anticipation, joy, and generosity—yes, all four. But I cannot justify taking such a step on both fronts at the same time. What should I do?*

Zach worked to regain his focus, and he successfully cranked out the framework for the final two pages. He found himself in a tremendous internal battle. Be courageous and generous with his funds in order to go to Haiti, or apply the same heart motivations related to proposing to Maggie?

He decided to click away from his work on the Haitian blessing proposal— give it time to simmer on the back burner for a few hours. Zach decided to focus on several of his other projects as well as his list of get-out-of-town tasks.

At the top of his TO-DO list was: *ask Alex to golf—for some mild January day.*

Zach had realized—based on the previous week's conversations with Larry—that he needed to make this a stronger priority if he were going to actively, authentically re-engage with his passion for sharing Christ in his workplace. He composed a quick e-mail to Alex, inviting him to golf, and he hit send.

Shortly after lunch, Zach had a text from Maggie: "Hey, hope your Monday is wonderful. When are we getting together this week? How about Thursday—dinner and some last-minute shopping?" Zach shot a quick text back: "Sounds great! How about I pick you up at six?"

"Great!" Mags replied. "Just make sure you're driving my main man, Henry!"

Zach resumed work on the Haiti proposal—now with some renewed focus and a clearer head. Though he still wasn't certain of his decision, the initial financial shock and frustration had worn off. He made major headway on the proposal and, by mid-afternoon, he met up with Larry for a quick review. The boss loved it, and after supplying a few points of feedback, he signaled his hearty thumbs-up to Zach.

"Send it, Zachary! Nice work," Larry affirmed. "'Will be exciting to see what we hear back. What you've created certainly reflects bold thinking, a solid concept to generously work toward blessing people and advancing Christ's kingdom. Sincerely, well done—I like it. Now, we'll see what our mysterious challenger thinks of the idea." No indication had been given of when they might receive word of their challenger's verdict.

On Tuesday evening, Zach placed a call to Gram back in Ohio. Although they had chatted a few times since Thanksgiving, they needed to talk together about specific Christmas details.

"I'm very excited to see you, Gram. There's so much to catch up on together!"

"'Can't wait to see *you*, Zachary! We are all doing well here. What's new in your adventure?"

In previous conversations, Zach had told her about the gold bag, the treasure chest, as well as the curious symbol to cipher. She also knew that Zach had continued sensing real progress as he encountered the characters of Bethlehem, including greater discoveries of faith-filled courage, kingdom anticipation, a choice to rejoice, and gracious generosity.

"It's all been pretty amazing, Gram. Some big stuff has unfolded. I'll share even more details when I get in Friday evening. I plan to leave after work—probably mid-afternoon, so it will probably be late when I arrive. But this way, we'll have all of Christmas Eve together, as well as Christmas Day, and the rest of the long weekend."

"Any chance that Miss Maggie might grace us with her lovely presence?" Gram asked with a twinge of romantic tease in her voice. She could readily ascertain that Mags and Zach's relationship had been advancing in positive ways. "You know how much the whole clan—your cousins, Uncle Clyde, and even Marshall—well, we all missed her at Thanksgiving. We love seeing you, Zach, but Maggie really is something extra-special."

"I know, Gram," Zach chuckled. "Sounds like you guys would be fine if I just send her and I'll stay in Pennsylvania." He gave a hardy laugh. "Just teasing, Gram. I wholeheartedly agree. Unfortunately, I think she's headed to New Jersey to be with extended family. You know *I* sure would like her to come, but I'm not certain how keen her fam' would be on that. After all, it's Christmas."

In the back of his mind, Zach was toying with laying out his grand dilemma for Gram. *Do I use the money I've saved to put down a deposit for Haiti, OR should I bite the bullet and buy an engagement ring? Perhaps Gram would have some wisdom.* Taking a big gulp, he braced to bring up the topic—when Gram suddenly cut things short.

"Okay, Zach, I know you've got big things to do, places to go, and people to see, so I'll let you go for now. I can't wait to have you home. Give me a shout when you're taking off on Friday afternoon."

"Will do, Gram. Love you, and can't wait to see you!"

Part of Zach regretted not bringing it up sooner, but a part of him was relieved to avoid the awkward discussion. And, after all, he was pretty sure he already knew what his decision was going to be.

CHAPTER 24

X Marks the Spot

Zach rolled up in front of Mags' place in the G37 at six o'clock sharp. She jumped in.

"Where's my boy? What gives?" Mags asked with a slight edge of annoyance in her voice.

"What are you talking about?" Zach fired back. "I'm here, and I'm even on time."

"No—where's Henry? I thought I was clear—you had to drive him. He's overdue for a checkup on his tailgate condition. 'Wondering how that wreath bandage is holding up."

"Oh, I totally forgot, Mags. Seriously, it was a total mental lapse. I drove the G37 to work this morning. I ran home quick to change clothes, and then the car was already there in the driveway, so I jumped right back in to come get you. Seriously, I'm sorry."

"Okay, I might forgive you," she teased.

Against Zach's better judgment, he agreed to go to the King of Prussia Mall. He had warned: "It'll be a madhouse, Mags." She agreed, but promptly reflected back to him how much fun it could be to join all the other crazy people just a couple days before Christmas.

"There's something of a rush about the sea of humanity, the music, a vintage Santa sporting a genuine beard, and the generally marvelous mayhem. It's really a bunch of fun, Zach. Come on!" She had pleaded her case quite convincingly, and of course, she won.

"Where should we eat?" Zach asked. "I'm starving!"

"Of *course* you are, and don't think I don't know that you're just stalling, trying to put off venturing into the mall. I'm very aware of your tactics, Zachary David!"

"No, I'm being totally honest—my day was a mad-dash rush—I barely had time at lunch to munch down a little six-pack of those cheese crackers and a bottle of juice. I'm famished. And I'm in no mood for the food court."

"Okay, if that's how you're going to be about it, then you have to take me to Maggiano's Little Italy. It's been at least seven or eight months since I ate there. The menu is scrumptious and portions are huge. It's my final offer."

"Well, if you insist," Zach responded, "then I accept!" It was plentiful banter, ripe with flirtation between them.

Entering the jam-packed lobby, they put in their names and discovered a two-hour wait for seating. "It's only a Thursday, not even the weekend!" Zach complained to Mags.

"Yes, but it's the holidays—busiest time of the year on this patch of property—and everyone has the same great idea—eat and shop. C'mon, let's go over to the mall. Shop for a bit. Then we'll come back to feast in a couple hours. And we'll buy you a snack if you're *truly* dying of hunger."

After walking the mall for ninety minutes, they landed back at Maggiano's and were soon settled into a back corner booth. The restaurant's Christmas décor included bright red gifts atop the pillars and candle lamps on each table. Drinks were ordered. Warm bread arrived, along with a scrumptious dipping sauce of olive oil, fresh ground pepper, and sprinkled Parmesan. Mags ordered Rigatoni D and Zach ordered four-cheese ravioli.

As they dove into their meals, Zach and Mags reflected on how delicious their pasta tasted, the joyous sounds of jazzy Christmas tunes, a thick aroma of zesty cheese, and the overall buzz of chatter filling the air.

"Oh, wow!" Mags interjected. "'Just remembered: last year at Christmastime, I was here with some friends on a Friday night. All of a sudden, we heard cheering and clapping over at that set of long tables." She was pointing across the restaurant. "A couple had just gotten engaged. Spontaneously, all of their friends plus everyone else in this place started applauding. It was seriously beautiful!" Maggie stared wistfully.

It was obvious to Zach there were visions of diamonds dancing in her head. If there had been any doubt in Zach's head that she would love to be engaged, this very moment erased any ounce of wondering. He needed to change the subject, and change it quickly.

"Say, I had a fantastic realization—a new thought hit me last night pertaining to the box lid's symbol, the *XP* cipher that Doc Ben interpreted for us."

"What's that?" Mags was sufficiently distracted from her dreams of bling.

"Well, remember how Doc explained that it stands for Christ?" Zach shared excitedly. "It's the first two letters of Christ's name in Greek. And it indicates his kingly fulfillment, right?"

"Yes, that's what he said," Mags agreed.

"So the thought hit me. My Uncle Clyde was making his big deal about people not removing Christ from Christmas, and he told me about the Christmas tree sales stand that simply advertised 'Xmas Trees for Sale.'"

"Sure, you told me about it. Anybody writing Merry Xmas seems to work up his righteous—or not-so-righteous—indignation." They both started chuckling.

"For my uncle, that ranks up there with people saying 'Happy Holidays.' Based on his attitude, he might as well say, 'Bah humbug!' But here's what hit me: those tree stands actually have it RIGHT! They're not marking Christ out. Anyone who proclaims Christmas that way is actually combining Jesus' royal symbol with the missional reference. We are sent people, actively commissioned for his royal mission of reaching more people and changing the world for his glory."

Mags was grinning as Zach shared. She took a big bite from the warm, caramel-drizzled brownie they were sharing. "That's a tremendous correlation, for sure, Zach. But that symbol now reminds me of something else." She had a twinkle in her eye.

"What's that?" Zach asked, puzzling at what her new, deep discovery might be.

"The first time you saw it, you said, 'X marks the spot,' and you talked about buried treasure. Do you remember?"

"I do. That was just my knee-jerk first thought when I saw it."

"Well, the *X* just makes me think, 'X marks the spot,' and 'cross my heart.'" She grinned, winked, and swiped her forefinger over her heart. "X marks the spot, and my heart belongs to you."

Zach blushed and scrambled for how to respond.

Not missing a beat, Mags came to his rescue. "Of course, there's a whole lot more. The *XP* also reminds me that Christ is our King and we must keep putting him at the very center of all we do, our relationship together, all of our work endeavors, and our ongoing quest to be workplace missionaries. We can love genuinely—X marks the spot—because he is our King."

Now Zach was smiling and oh-so-grateful she had changed the conversation. He debated whether he should be open and disclose his own internal turmoil over his financial dilemma—*engagement band or Haiti trip*. He came very close to telling her, but he just couldn't go there. Instead, he brought up Christmas plans.

They headed to the lobby, grabbed mints, and spun through the wooden revolving door. A very chilly, rather rainy and somewhat icy mix was falling at a steady pace. Conversation continued as the G37 was warming up.

"So I'm headed to Gram's tomorrow. You know, Mags, everyone there is asking if you're coming."

She sported a giant smile. "Everyone there, eh? Is there anyone *here* who is asking?" Suddenly, Maggie was blushing a bit, as if she just realized she was being quite bold in her overtures this evening.

"Your dad said you're headed to New Jersey to see family. I'd love you to come, seriously. You light the place up when you're with all of us at Gram's. But your dad—"

Zach put the G37 in reverse and began slowly backing out of the parking spot.

"I know," Mags interjected. "Those *are* the plans. Dad more than implied that I should join them since I was elsewhere for Thanksgiving." Zach knew all too well about the elsewhere and *who* went with that elsewhere. *Argggg! Did I really ask him to golf with me in January?* The dark shadows of his jealousy were engulfing him again.

Just then—*SLAM. Crunch!* Seemingly out of nowhere, they were clobbered from the back. It was a zooming incoming Mercedes.

Zach and Mags felt the impact and the sound of collision. Fortunately, no airbags deployed and they felt no bodily harm.

Climbing out and walking to the back, they encountered the results—the G37's rear end was a mess. Taillight and back bumper were crushed, and shards of red lens covered the pavement. The driver's side fender was pushed into the tire, which was punctured and bulging. Apparently, the Mercedes' driver was in too much of a hurry and failed to get stopped on the slick asphalt.

"You've got to be kidding! Just my dumb luck," Zach growled. "And right before I'm supposed to drive to Gram's tomorrow."

"Well, it looks like Henry is headed over the river and through the woods." Mags laughed at her wittiness. "Christmas at Grandmother's house—hurrah for Henry!"

CHAPTER 25

The First Gift of Christmas

Firing up his computer on Friday morning, Zach plunged into the final items on his get-out-of-town list. He was aiming to be on the road by noon, assuming he could conquer his ambitious lineup of tasks.

He called the insurance company in an attempt to start the claim on the G37.

He composed three e-mails, quick status reports for developers on various projects set to commence in January.

Last-minute Christmas cards were personalized for about a dozen clients and several of their partnering engineers.

Finally, Zach mustered the courage to revisit James' e-mail. Finding the link, he clicked on the Haiti trip registration form. Stroking the keys, he filled in his details, including his necessary bank account information. Deep in his heart, Zach knew this was the right priority choice. He was personally applying gracious generosity toward Christ's mission—a step he was determined to take at a new level.

He knew his love for Mags was strong, so he felt the ongoing tension and personal pull toward buying a ring. *But I just know this is the right decision for this season. I have limited resources, and I know I need to go to Haiti to discover more about God's work there.* Zach gulped, grinned, and clicked on SUBMIT. He proceeded to compose a quick e-mail to James, updating him on his excitement over joining the team.

"Hey, Zach!" Larry was standing at his office door. It was mid-morning. "A courier just dropped this at the front desk."

It was a simple letter, thanking them for submitting their proposal. "Our final decision to award will be made and communicated by January 15. We thank you for your interest and your thoughtful work toward being a blessing in God's work in this world. Merry Xmas!"

"Wow. That makes it sound like there are still multiple candidates," Zach responded with a distinct tone of disappointment. "And I guess I hoped I would know something before Christmas."

"Yes, I agree," Larry responded, "but often we run into our own wishful thinking—even overcalculated expectations—and life rolls at a slower pace than we envisioned."

Zach nodded. "I'm encountering that on multiple fronts these days. But I do like how our friend signed off with 'Merry

Xmas." Zach proceeded to explain why, evoking a solid chuckle of agreement from Larry.

Zach and Henry hit the road for Ohio about one o'clock. Zach patted Henry's tailgate and noted his still-green wreath. Their drive was relatively uneventful. No Bubba or Godzilla truck this time. Once he had safely sailed through Bellville, Zach felt compelled to call Gram for a quick "all's good" bulletin.

He arrived at Gram's a little after nine o'clock. They chatted updates together over hot tea, including his latest correlations about the *XP* symbol and he and Mags' adventures. Zach even opened up to share his personal turmoil—engagement ring versus trip to Haiti.

"I have to say, Zachary, that's a very faith-filled decision. And you can trust God to provide. He will be faithful. If the Father could provide gold, frankincense, and myrrh for Mary, Joseph, and Jesus, I think he can supply a shiny rock and little band of gold for you and Mags when the time is right."

Zach grinned. "I hope you're right, and I believe you are, Gram. I believe you're *exactly* right!" Gram poured more tea as she nodded.

"And you know, Gram, it has truly been a remarkable season, especially when I think about how I felt four weeks ago. I was so dismal and discouraged, really not looking forward to Christmas, not at all. While Uncle Clyde can seem very quirky, he was precisely on-target. My interaction with the old

Christmas characters has brought me a sharpened grasp and real-to-life personal discoveries of faith-filled courage and kingdom anticipation—it's why I'm so compelled to explore and get involved in Haiti. And I've gained a greater level of jubilant joy as well as new levels of generosity."

Their daytime schedule for Christmas Eve included some last-minute shopping and giftwrapping. Gram was very grateful for Zach's extra hands to lend such wrapping help, as well as his assistance in preparing for the roast beef feast. Family and friends stopped by late afternoon, including various cousins, Uncle Clyde, Marshall from next door—even Doc Ben popped in for just a few minutes. The whole gang indulged in roasted carrots and potatoes, pickled olives, warm-from-the-oven rolls, and the delectable "roast beast." Zach had dubbed their traditional meal by that nickname as a kid, mimicking Dr. Seuss' famous lines from *the Grinch*.

The whole gaggle of family and friends attended the seven o'clock Christmas Eve service together. It was a glowing service, including carols, reflective readings, and the traditional candle lighting with the closing song, *Silent Night*. As the pastor dismissed the crowd, Zach noted words of blessing and strong encouragement to share the King's all-out joy with family and friends across the coming days.

He was deeply reflecting. *Immense thanks to you, Lord. Tonight's service punctuated my entire Bethlehem journey. With this Christmas Eve, I seriously sense your missa. Like never before, I can say I've been to mass.* Zach chuckled at his own internal Protestant humor. *I am sent out to generously share your grace! Thank you, King Jesus.* He was recalling his Latin and Greek lessons of recent weeks.

Those attending were stunned as they exited the service, but no one was more delighted than Zachary: it was snowing! Not rain, not sleet or ice, not even of hint of anything close to a wintry mix. It was all-out, full-fledged snow.

Zach and Gram drove home very carefully. As Henry rolled down the white, blanketed roads, Zach wished so much that Mags was here to see this. *She would LOVE this!* And he made a further mental note. *Take a picture of Henry's snow-covered tailgate and wreath. Make certain to text it to her later. She'll love it.*

They arrived home and started to settle in. The house would refill with family on Christmas morning, but the rest of the evening would be just Zach and Gram. There was a bit of wrapping and baking to finish, but it was sure to be a quiet evening. Gram started brewing a fresh pot of hot tea.

"Hey, Zachary. Come here a minute." Gram was calling from the living room.

"What do you need? I'm coming, just a minute," Zach replied.

He entered from the kitchen. Gram was standing next to the glowing Christmas tree. "I think Santa must have done an early stop at our house while we were over at the service."

Gram was grinning something of a mischievous look. "I spy a little package tucked up here." She pointed into an up-high branch. She had a tradition of giving a "first gift of Christmas." When Zach was just a child, he and his cousins typically received pajamas or storybooks. Over the years, Gram's gifts for Christmas Eve had become a bit more grownup, yet still typically rather down-to-earth, often humorous and altogether practical.

Zachary searched and quickly found a very small shimmery box with a bow. He lifted it from the branches and smiled. "Now what is this?" he exclaimed as he held it and stared at her.

"Go ahead. Open it. No need to delay," Gram coaxed.

Zach fumbled his fingers, finding the edges on the tiny package. Tearing away the paper and opening the box lid, he was stunned. It was an antique engagement ring.

"Gram, what in the world!?" It was not a real question—Zach knew this was her diamond and band, given to her by Grandpa back when she was just eighteen years old. Zach had admired it from the time he was small. Though it was a classic setting, the diamond was as brilliant and clear as ever. Family and friends had admired it as a stunningly crafted design.

Zach was shaking his head. "There's no way, Gram. I can't accept this. Grandpa gave—"

Gram cut him off. "Yes, you can. *I* want you to accept this, and I know your grandfather would want you take it, just like he wanted you to have Henry. You and Mags can certainly get the diamond reset in a newer setting if you'd like."

"Oh, my word, Gram, thank you *so* much. I don't know what else to say."

"Nothing else you need to say to me, young man. It's what you need to say to a certain Miss Maggie. That's what you need to start thinking about." Gram laughed, and Zach joined in with her tease.

They went back to the kitchen. Pouring the tea, they noticed it was still snowing, now at an even heavier pace. Gram began pulling out ingredients for her two pies. Several times in a row Gram's phone chirped, indicating that she had a text. That jogged Zach's memory, and he sent his picture of Henry's snow-dusted tailgate and wreath. He told Gram what he was sending to Mags. Gram lifted her eyebrows and smiled. "Oh, yes, she'll love that. 'Will make her wish she was here to enjoy the white Christmas along with Henry and all of us."

Zach asked for a review of how Grandpa had proposed to Gram all those years ago. After a recap of the story, Zachary headed to the back bedroom for a few final gifts that needed to be wrapped. All of a sudden, he heard Gram calling again.

"Zachary, 'better come out here!"

What's Gram want now? Zach mused under his breath. *'Really need to get these presents wrapped so I'm not still up at midnight.* "I'm coming!" He headed back to the kitchen.

Gram was peering out the kitchen door window. "Someone just pulled in. 'Think you better head out there. 'Might be someone needing help in the snow."

Zach bundled up and glanced through the door's glass. It was not a familiar car, but it had parked right behind Henry. He stepped onto the patio—snow was falling even heavier than before—and the strange visitor had climbed out of the car and lifted the trunk. Gram's driveway had a single lamppost, and the heavy blowing snow made it impossible for Zach to see clearly.

He confidently headed toward the car, envisioning it was someone in need of a snow scraper or wiper fluid.

"Hello there," Zach called across the driveway. "Can I help you?"

"Certainly you can! You can carry my bag and these presents!"

It was Mags. As Zach came closer, her red scarf was more visible. And she was sporting a gigantic "I-gotcha" smile.

"Oh, my word! What are you doing here? No way!" Zach was overwhelmed with excitement. Instead of picking up her bags, he picked *her* up in his arms and whirled her around. Like glimpsing into a snow globe, the now-cascading flakes were creating an all-out idyllic wonderland.

Mags had come straight from the airport. In her excitement at arrival, she had left the rental car's headlights on. They were shining brightly against Henry's tailgate. She grabbed Zach's hands and tugged him over to stand with her between the two vehicles. In the glow of the headlights that were illuminating Henry's wreath, they kissed. It was an all-out adoring kiss, the kind of Christmas kiss that finally settled things in Zach's mind once and for all. She certainly loved Zach way more than old Henry.

"Does Gram know you're coming?"

"Of course she does. We've been texting all afternoon. You don't think I'd just show up unannounced, do you?" Mags laughed and hugged him tighter.

"I still don't get it," Zach said with great puzzlement in his voice. "Your dad, and New Jersey, and—"

"Now Zachary David," Maggie replied. "You know how my dad operates. He made those plans, but then this morning he asked me, 'Where do you really want to be, in your heart of hearts, Mags, this Christmas?'"

"And I told him, 'Well, Dad, if X marks the spot,' and I swiped my fingers over my heart just like this, 'well, you know exactly where I belong this Christmas.'"

Advent Week 4: Reflections and Exercises
on Gracious Generosity

1. When have you encountered an especially generous Christmas gift? Share about that experience and how you felt/responded.

2. Explore Matthew 2:1–12. What do you discover about the wise men's joy and generosity?

3. What do you think of the three thick threads—"move past charity, mark them with dignity and sustainability?" How would you describe each? How do you see this approach as unique and potentially more fruitful for generosity and mission?

4. With family or a group of friends, watch the classic movie *A Christmas Carol*. Discuss together how the characters, especially Scrooge, emerged with greater joy and generosity.

5. What might it look like for your own workplace to engage in more creative giving of time, finances, and/or service to others? Consider leading and joining coworkers in making fresh generosity goals for these final days of Advent and for the opening months of the New Year.

6. Identify one or two tangible steps you and your family or friends might take during this season to be more generous.

7. Across these weeks, how have you related to the old Christmas characters—like Mary, Joseph, shepherds, and

wise men? What have been your personal discoveries regarding faith-filled courage, kingdom anticipation, jubilant joy, and gracious generosity?

8. How do you anticipate the story of Henry's Christmas might have a positive effect on your work perspective and actions, both at Christmas and all year long?

NEXT-STEP RESOURCES

When Helping Hurts: How to Alleviate Poverty without Hurting the Poor... and Yourself, by Steve Corbett and Brian Fikkert (Moody, 2012)

Joy for the World: How Christianity Lost Its Cultural Influence and Can Begin Rebuilding It, by Greg Forster (Crossway, 2014)

Be You. Do Good. Having the Guts to Pursue What Makes You Come Alive, by Jonathan David Golden (Baker, 2016)

The Gospel Goes to Work: God's Big Canvas of Calling and Renewal, by Stephen R. Graves (Edit Resource, 2015)

Right Here Right Now: Everyday Mission for Everyday People, by Alan Hirsch and Lance Ford (Baker 2011)

Entrepreneurship for Human Flourishing, by Chris Horst and Peter Greer (American Enterprise Institute, 2014)

God Came Near, by Max Lucado (Multnomah, 1987)

The MacArthur New Testament Commentary: Matthew 1–7, by John MacArthur, Jr. (Moody, 1985)

The Real Mary: Why Evangelical Christians Can Embrace the Mother of Jesus, by Scot McKnight (Paraclete, 2007)

Workplace Grace: Becoming a Spiritual Influence at Work, by Bill Peel and Walt Larimore (LeTourneau, 2014)

ACKNOWLEDGEMENTS

I am so deeply grateful to my wife, Nancy, and my three sons, Jarod, Joel, and Josiah. Your love and encouragement make our adventures as a family—including the creation of a resource such as this—so much sweeter!

I am forever indebted to my mother, Holly, for intentionally sharing with me her love for books and for crafting intriguing tales. Thanks, Mom, for making it such a priority to read stories to me, even as a wiggly toddler.

My utmost appreciation goes out to the marvelous team of staff, leaders, and friends throughout Manor Church. Your ever-growing commitment to actively integrate your faith in your everyday workplaces supplies ongoing impetus for designing and sharing resources like this one.

I am extremely grateful to Rick and the team at CrossLink, for your excellence and enthusiasm to create empowering tools that bless others and advance Christ's work.

And most importantly, I offer up highest praise and thanks to our King and Savior, Jesus Christ. Your coming to earth and your sending us out on your kingdom mission are the very heartbeat of these pages and all of Christmas!

ABOUT THE AUTHOR

John Elton Pletcher is crazy about connecting with people over delicious coffee. He also enjoys running, watching movies, reading, playing baseball with his boys, and taking long walks with his golden retriever, Brodimus Maximus.

John serves as lead pastor at Manor Church in Lancaster, Pennsylvania, and also teaches as adjunct faculty at Eastern University and Evangelical Seminary. He is married to Nancy, and they have three sons, Jarod, Joel and Josiah.

Pletch, as friends call him, holds a Doctor of Ministry in Leadership from Denver Seminary and a Master of Divinity from Clarks Summit University.

John's first book is *Henry's Glory: A Story for Discovering Lasting Significance in Your Daily Work* (Wipf and Stock, 2013). He also coauthored *EmotiConversations: Working through Our Deepest Places* (Wipf and Stock, 2016) with his mother, Holly Hall-Pletcher.

Passionate about helping leaders develop bigger hearts and skills for missional living, he is available for consultation, coaching, storytelling, and conference/seminar speaking.

For further information about scheduling John for your event, plus reading his engaging blog and other creative resources, visit johneltonpletcher.com.